D1631977

Prepare yourself, dear reader, for you are about to enter the strange and mystical world of DAN RHODES, THE MAGIC...

(OK, that's probably a bit on the dramatic side. Let's start again, shall we?)

Hi! My name is Dan Rhodes, and I've been obsessed with magic since I was seven years old.

(Much, much better!)

Now, magic comes in many different forms, shapes and sizes, as you'll soon discover with each page of this book you turn. However, my book isn't just about illusions and magic tricks (although I promise there are quite a lot of them!) I'm also going to tell you all about me, Dan Rhodes - about how I got started in magic, how magic changed my life, about my social media journey, my friends and family, my influences and heroes, and how I eventually gained millions of subscribers and followers online. Plus, I'm going to share my tips, tricks and secrets to help you do the same! I hope you're ready for all that!

To me, the best thing about magic is how it can bring people together, and that anyone can understand and enjoy it - young or old, and from anywhere in the world. It has no barriers or boundaries - it's just MAGIC!

Enjoy!

First published in 2022 by HEADLINE PUBLISHING GROUP
a division of HACHETTE UK

978 1 4722 9474 6

Printed and bound in Italy by LEGO S. p. A.
Colour reproduction by AltaImage London
Main photography © Laurie Fletcher
Personal photographs provided by Dan and Lisa Rhodes
Design by Dan Newman and Isobel Gillan

Page 30 © Suzan Moore / Alamy, page 46 © Robert Wallace / Wallace M Moore
/ Alamy, page 73 (middle and bottom) © Ruth Meredith Photography, page 78
© London Entertainment / Alamy, page 82 © WENN / Alamy, page 150
© John Henshall / Alamy, page 172 © Xinhua / Alamy.

HEADLINE PUBLISHING GROUP

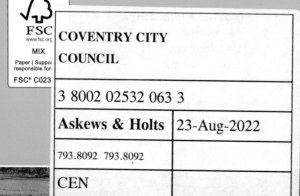

CONTENTS

For my amazing
Grandad Stephen

x

A MAGIC MOMENT

Whenever you watch a magic trick being performed, there's always an amazing moment. A moment of pure astonishment, just after the trick happens, before you start wondering how on earth it was done or questioning what your eyes may have missed. It's that moment when you see something happen and actually believe that magic exists. It's a split second of genuine astonishment when everything you ever thought real has been flipped on its head.

It's especially true when you experience that moment as a kid, when magic is something you still believe in. It was in one of those moments that I fell in love with the idea of magic and the feeling that anything is possible. And I wanted to make that magic happen!

If you think about it, there are so many different types of people in the world. Some are cheerful and bubbly, some are serious or moody, some are confident, others are shy. Still, when you show somebody a magic trick, it doesn't matter who they are, or what their personality, their reaction is almost always a positive, happy one. You can leave some people speechless with a magic trick. Others might go crazy and start shouting out in disbelief. Either way, it's a reaction saying, How has that just happened? Can I actually believe my eyes? Was that for real?

That was definitely the feeling I got the first time I saw a magic trick. To this day, that feeling is something that has never left me. Magic can still take me back to the feeling of being a little kid again. That's why it's been my mission to pass on that special feeling to other people, to make them truly experience the same wonder that I felt, and still feel, when somebody makes magic. It's what I love most about performing tricks, watching the different reactions I get from my audience. I think it's what you will love about showing people the tricks in this book too.

Another thing I love about the art of magic is that there's a secret to every trick. Every single one. There are usually many moving parts that have to come together, like pieces of a puzzle, to create the final trick or illusion. It's one of the reasons that I think that teaching people magic tricks is a good thing – if they want to learn – because most of the time, the secret is more impressive than the trick itself! But (and it's a big but) you have to be careful not to give all your secrets away. That's very important. In fact, if you do one of the tricks from this book and somebody asks, 'Wow! How did you do that?' just answer, 'Very well,' and leave it there! Or ask them if they can keep a secret and when they tell you they can, say, 'Well, so can I!' Usually, one of those two snappy replies will be enough to shut them down, or at least get a laugh.

But letting you into some of my secrets was one of the reasons I was so keen to write this book – so I can share the things I've learned along the way, and I can show you, my readers and budding magicians, the secrets behind the tricks. Well, some of them anyway – not all of them! Some things are better left a mystery.

THE BEGINNING

I was born in Rochdale near Manchester on 23 June 2003, four weeks sooner than I was supposed to. I reckon I was just keen to get out into the world and get going. I struggled to breathe for a while so I spent the first two weeks of my life in an intensive-care ward for sick or premature babies, but after that, I was able to leave the hospital and go home.

Back then we lived in an area of Rochdale called Milnrow. It's a small but lovely village with old-fashioned cottages, a few shops and a pub or two. We lived in a nice four-bedroomed detached house – not that I remember much about it myself, because we moved when I was about eighteen months old. Our next house was in a village further towards the Pennines called Walsden. It was still just a village, but a bigger one – as was the house we lived in, which had five bedrooms! Moving up in life – ha ha!

There always seemed to be lots going in our house when I was little. Everyone was on the go. My mum, Lisa, and dad, Simon, both worked full time, so I went to a nursery, like my older brother, Harrison. Twice a week, sometimes three times, my gran would pick us up after nursery, and we'd go back to her and Grandad's house for tea. They only lived a couple of miles away from us, so I saw quite a lot of them – we were always very close. My gran's mum – Granny Margaret – was also close by, in fact she lived right next door to Gran and Grandad, which meant we could pop round on our own whenever we wanted to see her. Gran and Grandad had a sandwich shop and café called Greenwood's in Rochdale. They made delicious bacon and egg butties, so they definitely knew

how sort us out with a decent tea before Mum picked us up on her way back from work. Sometimes during school holidays, when Harrison and I were a bit older, we'd hang out at the café. I'd put on an apron and then take the orders to give to my gran. I even did magic tricks for some of the customers for tips. I have always been very industrious!

I was only three years old when things started to change, and my mum and dad split up. Harrison was seven at the time, so I'm sure he probably remembers more about it than I do. All I know is that suddenly my dad wasn't living with us anymore, although we still saw him regularly.

I know that, for some kids, the break-up of their parents' marriage can feel like the worst thing imaginable. I suppose I had a different way of seeing the world. I mean, if it's at all possible, I'll always try to flip things to a positive. Growing up, I just thought it meant two lots of presents at birthdays and Christmas, and an extra holiday. We did go on some really cool holidays: Florida, Egypt, Cape Verde, Mexico . . . I was very lucky in that respect. Mum tells me that she never got to go on lovely holidays when she was a kid; my dad didn't either. So, they wanted to make sure we went on some fantastic trips and got to see the world. After my mum and dad split up, we still got to holiday with both our parents – only now it was separately. We always got to spend quality time with both Mum and Dad and as I got older, with more understanding of life, I realised that they were such very different people, and were much happier apart than they had been together.

I'LL ALWAYS TRY TO FLIP THINGS TO A POSITIVE

Harrison

ON DAN

The thing about Dan is, he never has a day off. I sometimes say to him, 'You need to wind down and just chill.'

'I can't,' he says. 'I've got this to do, or I've got that to achieve.'

I've never known Dan to be sitting there saying, 'I don't know what to do next.' He's always got some new idea on the go.

I think one of Dan's strong points is that he understands his audience. He's got a knack for knowing what kind of content will do well. He can usually predict the videos that are likely to go viral. I guess it's because he's put so much out there over a long period.

Eventually, Mum, Harrison and I moved to our house in Shaw, not far out of Manchester, between Oldham and Rochdale – I think I was about five or six by then – and that's where I've lived ever since. Back then, my life was quite ordinary and structured really: get up, breakfast, school, playtime, tea, bath, bed. No different from any other kid in any other family.

Mum tells me that, as a young child, I was highly sociable – always talking and trying to get in on the action. But, when I first went to school,

I STILL WASN'T MIXING WITH OTHER KIDS OR JOINING IN

that changed. At a parents' evening when I was in reception class, Mum was shocked to hear what the teacher had to say about me.

'Daniel's very quiet. He doesn't talk to the other kids or join in with anything. Basically, it's like he's in his own little world.'

'Are you sure you got the right kid? Daniel Rhodes?' Mum said, a bit confused. 'You do know whose mum I am, don't you?' This definitely didn't seem like a description of the noisy, chatty kid she'd bought up for the last four years. No way!

Her first thought was that I was missing the teachers I'd got to know back at nursery, so she arranged for them to pay me a visit at the new school. That way, they could check up on me and see how I was getting on in a new environment. My nursery teachers seemed to think everything was OK on the day they were there, but as the school year went on, I still wasn't mixing with other kids or joining in with games or activities. it was sometimes hard for me to weigh up or read certain situations as quickly as other people did. The only people I engaged with were the teachers and other adults. And even then, I couldn't seem to concentrate on lessons or anything else I should be focusing on.

Someone suggested I might be dyslexic, and that might be what was making me so withdrawn. So I ended up getting some extra help with my school work and a lot of one-to-one tuition. But when I was assessed to find out if I did have dyslexia the outcome was that I didn't have it after all, so suddenly, all the extra help and tuition I was getting disappeared. Not good! Mum tells me that I'd come on in leaps and bounds while I was getting the extra tuition, but that once it was over, I started falling behind again. Most of the time, I was off in my own little dream world, not listening to what the teachers said and not moving forward with my education.

There was obviously another reason. It was something my mum had to find out the hard way! In the end, the school suggested that she get a referral from our doctor for some more evaluations, which is what she did. That's when she was told that I had something called Asperger's Syndrome. It was explained to her that it was a disorder that affects a person's natural development. They told her that people with Asperger's find it tough to relate to others in a social situation, and their behaviour and thinking patterns tend to be rigid and repetitive. On the other side of the coin, they're often gifted or artistic in some way, can be very determined when it comes to achieving goals and also tend to be quite straightforward and loyal. So there was likely to be a lot of positive stuff that would go hand-in-hand with the negative.

> MOST OF THE TIME, I WAS OFF IN MY OWN LITTLE DREAM WORLD, NOT LISTENING TO WHAT THE TEACHERS SAID

Once Mum had the diagnosis, she realised she'd seen signs of it in the past. Like how when I focused on a specific task or thing, I couldn't move on until that task or that want, or question was satisfied. Being so inquisitive and persistent was both a blessing and a curse. In a sense, it was good for getting the answers I was looking for, but could sometimes come across as nagging and annoying.

One of the cool holidays we went on was a trip to Lapland with my mum and brother. It was just a long weekend, Friday to Monday, in early December, but I absolutely loved it there and didn't want to come home. Of course, being that time of year, there was a trip to meet Santa included. I'd already written him a letter telling him that one of the things I wanted was some superhero superpowers. I'm sure there were probably some other things I wanted, but I remember that being the main one.

Once I was there, in the presence of Santa, I mentioned again that superpowers were at the very top of my Christmas list. Santa assured me that I would get some. My mum, meanwhile, was thinking, 'Well, he isn't going to get *that* present!' But she assumed that by Christmas I'd have forgotten all about it anyway. Wrong! I also took things very literally. If someone told me something, I believed it to be true. As far as I was concerned, we'd gone all the way to Lapland to visit Santa, so yes! I was getting my superpowers! Whether anyone liked it or not!

On Christmas Eve, while all the family gathered at our house for the big day, I marched into the kitchen to see my mum.

'I can't wait till tomorrow! I can't wait to get my superhero powers so I can fly from my bedroom, down the stairs to the living room.'

I could see Mum getting this concerned look in her eye, like she needed to tell me something but she wasn't sure how to. As it turned out, her concern was because my bedroom was on the third floor of the house, so flying down from it was going to be quite a challenge for a six-year-old boy, or anyone really.

Knowing how literally I always took things, Mum had to sit me down and explain that Santa had been in contact with her to tell her that, unfortunately, he was all out of superpowers so I wouldn't be getting any that year. She knew only too well that if she hadn't told me that, there was a good chance I'd end up in A&E on Christmas Day after throwing myself down the stairs, expecting to fly like Superman!

Something I did get from Santa one Christmas was a magic kit, which I ended up playing with non-stop. In fact, it came to be my favourite present of all that year. I really got into it, teaching myself as many tricks as I possibly could before trying them out on my poor unsuspecting family. That was good enough for me – not quite superpowers but my friends at school didn't know the difference. They were convinced I was a real-life superman. It would be a while before I really started getting obsessed with magic, but that magic set was most definitely the spark!

SOMETHING I DID GET FROM SANTA ONE CHRISTMAS WAS A MAGIC KIT, WHICH I ENDED UP PLAYING WITH NON-STOP

23

MAGIC
OBSESSED

If things had gone a bit differently, I might have ended up becoming a ventriloquist instead of a magician. Not long before I got that first magic set, while we were in Egypt, I saw a performer by the name of Gareth Oliver. He was doing his very first gig at the holiday resort where we were staying. I remember being blown away by how clever the art of ventriloquism was. Channelling your voice into puppet. Talking without moving your lips!

As well as being a really talented ventriloquist, Gareth also had a love for magic. I hung out with him a few times while we were on that holiday. Gareth did this magic trick where he made a coin go through the bottom of an upturned glass. I was amazed at what I'd witnessed. I spent the next hour in my room, hitting a coin against the bottom of a glass, trying my absolute hardest to make it happen for me. I remember my mum coming in while I banged coin against glass over and over again – I wasn't giving up.

'Dan, be careful – you'll smash it and cut yourself if you keep on doing that,' she said. But I didn't want to stop until I'd mastered it, which, of course, I couldn't.

Once I'd seen it, I couldn't get the trick out of my mind. I spent the entire trip thinking about it. It wasn't just the fact that it was an impressive trick; it was the feeling I got witnessing something like that with my own eyes – something magic. How was it possible? What was the secret? The whole thing sent this feeling of wonder and astonishment through me. It was one of those magic moments.

After Gareth's last show before we left the resort, he finally showed me how the trick was done. Yes, I was blown away, but there was something else. The best part about it was that there really was

a secret to it. I loved the idea that in order to do the trick, I had to know something that nobody else knew!

The following year, I saw Gareth performing on a cruise, and after that, I got my very own ventriloquist's puppet. There's a great old family photo of me opening that gift with a look of absolute joy on my face.

In the end, however, magic was bound to win out over ventriloquism. I think the real turning point for me came on that same cruise. The resident magician brought me up on stage to assist him with a trick.

'Hi, what's your name?' he asked as I stepped up.

'Dan.'

'And how old are you, Dan?'

'Seven.'

> I LOVED THE IDEA THAT IN ORDER TO DO THE TRICK, I HAD TO KNOW SOMETHING THAT NOBODY ELSE KNEW!

'Well,' he said, 'you have to be nine to do this trick, so how old are you again?'

'Seven,' I said again.

'Yes, Dan, but remember I said you have to be nine to do the trick. So, how old are you?'

'Seven.' (As I told you, I took everything quite literally as a kid!)

This went on for a while. By then, the audience were all laughing, thinking I was up there being hilarious. Actually, the fact that he was trying to get me to say I was nine just went over my head. I just took the question at face value, so I didn't take the hint.

'So how old are you, Dan?' He said for, like, the tenth time.

People in the audience started calling out.

'NINE! JUST SAY NINE!'

DYNAMO

Dynamo really is my hero of heroes, as far as magic goes. Born in Bradford, his real name is Steven Frayne, but he got the name Dynamo when he was an up-and-coming magician performing in New York in the early 2000s – at an event to commemorate the famous escapologist, Houdini. The audience was full of top magicians, including David Blaine and David Copperfield, and mid-way through his performance someone shouted from the audience, 'This kid is a dynamo!' and it stuck!

I first discovered him through his *Magician Impossible* TV series. Since that first TV show, the great man has toured the world – his *Seeing Is Believing* arena tour was seen by over 750,000 people – and he was the first magician ever to play the O2 in London! Of course, it isn't just his brilliant sleight-of-hand tricks he's known for, there are also all his amazing feats like walking on water, stepping through glass or freezing water in a fountain, amongst many, many others.

Through his books and interviews, I've learned so much about Dynamo over the years, and it turns out we have a few things in common as well as magic. Aside from also being a northern boy from a working-class background, he's accomplished all he has despite problems with his health.

When he was seventeen, he was diagnosed with Crohn's disease, which affects the stomach and digestive system. At the height of his career, doctors told him he might never be able to use his hands or perform magic ever again. His answer: 'I do the impossible, I'm not going to go out like this.'

Suddenly, the penny dropped.

'Nine!' I said, finally, and the whole of the audience jumped up and started cheering.

I suppose that was my first experience being in front of an audience with all eyes on me. And I'd be lying if I said I didn't love the attention. I've always been an attention seeker, to be honest!

With me on stage, the magician did a trick called The Floating Table, where he made a table hover inches above the ground and float in the air. I was astounded! When the table finally landed, he took a chocolate out of a box on the table and told me it was magical. Supposedly the chocolate had made the table float. Of course, I believed him. Funnily enough, it looked just like one of the chocolates that got left on my pillow each night of the cruise when they turned down the beds... As far as I was concerned, though, if the man who made a table float told me it was magic chocolate... then it was magic chocolate!

Not only did I keep that chocolate throughout the cruise, but I also took it home with me and kept it safe in my room. So, when I came home from school to find it had melted one day, I was devastated – crying my eyes out. Nightmare.

After the cruise, I felt like performing magic was something I absolutely had to learn so I could pass that feeling of wonder on to others. I wanted to astonish people. That was when my obsession really kicked in. Any spare time I had was spent watching back-to-back videos of Dynamo and David Blaine on YouTube. I learned almost all my tricks from watching YouTube tutorials, which is quite ironic considering I am now technically a YouTuber! But Dynamo was always my ultimate hero. He was performing blistering and fantastic magic to ordinary people in the street. It wasn't too much of a stretch

to imagine myself doing something like that. I wouldn't need a stage or even a paying audience; just myself, a pack of cards, and a few random strangers – all of that was easy to find!

Mum says magic was all I could talk about at one stage. When she tells me about it she says she and everyone else just couldn't get away from it, 'Magic was in my face 24/7! Magic tricks, one after another. It used to do my head in!' My poor family! I must have driven them crazy!

My Granny Margaret also fell victim to my relentless magic obsession. Whenever I went round to her place, I'd subject her to all my latest tricks, convincing myself that I was being fabulously entertaining. One day, Granny Margaret made a suggestion that threw me a bit.

MUM SAYS MAGIC WAS ALL I COULD TALK ABOUT

'Wouldn't you like to be a tennis player, Dan?' she said. 'Or a singer?

'What? What do you mean?'

'Oh, I think you'd make a great singer if you practised hard enough,' she said.

When I asked my mum why Granny Margaret had suggested I should be a singer or a tennis player, Mum told me, in the nicest possible way, that poor Granny Margaret was getting sick of me 'constantly doing magic tricks the whole time'.

'Oh, right!' I said, all grumpy. 'Well, whenever I go round to her house, she's got *Deal Or No Deal* on the telly, and I'm sick of that – but I wouldn't tell her to stop watching it!'

Grandad was a bit more receptive towards my budding magician skills. I could try a magic trick out on him ten or even twenty times without fear of him getting bored as I tried to get it right. He was always so patient and encouraging. Most people got fed up after I'd showed them eight or nine tricks (I can't think why!), but with Grandad, I could go on and on, and he always wanted to see more. He was always happy to sit there with me until I'd got the trick right. Bless him!

From there on in, it didn't matter what the setting was or the occasion; I was always up for doing some tricks. On a shopping trip to the supermarket when I was about eight, Mum turned around expecting to see me behind her, only to find that I'd disappeared. For a minute or so, she panicked and searched up and down the aisles of the supermarket, wondering what on earth could have happened for me to have vanished so completely. Then, suddenly, she spotted a great big circle of people gathered at the far end of the shop. As she headed down the aisle towards the crowd, she was saying to herself, 'Whatever this circle is, I just know Dan's in the middle of it.'

She was right! Lo and behold, there I was, with a big grin, performing an impromptu magic show for all the customers.

The funny thing was, there just so happened to be another magician in the crowd that day.

'He's terrific, your lad,' he told Mum. 'I've got some tricks that I could teach him if you'd like.'

I was lucky in that respect; I met quite a few magicians who were willing to show me new tricks, so I could continually build up my repertoire.

Back then, my dad's best friend was a guy I knew as Uncle Ste. He knew a load of card tricks, which he was happy to

teach me whenever we met up with him and his daughter at our weekly swimming lessons. If I'd mastered one trick by the following week, then he'd teach me another. I learned a lot from him. One of the first tricks he taught me was one I sometimes call The Crazy Aces, which you can learn on page 86. But before you try it, back to the story . . .

Aside from doing magic, I was really into performing as a kid, whether it was dancing, taking part in school plays, or just jumping on the karaoke machine at family gatherings. Basically, I was having fun doing something that came naturally to me. Anything that allowed me to 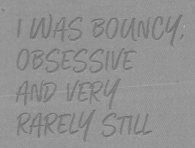 step into the limelight and express myself. I think I just loved all the attention at that age, and to be honest, I still do.

As primary school went on, and as I got a bit older, I stopped being the quiet, withdrawn child my reception teacher had told Mum about. I was bouncy, obsessive and very rarely still. I think I felt like I needed to be heard, so I was never shy about shouting out in class. I still wasn't that interested in the more academic stuff, and sometimes I struggled with maths and English. Funnily enough, I loved history and science, so those were the subjects I got into and focused a bit more on. As my teacher Miss Gardiner remembers, 'He was most definitely more enthusiastic about some things over others. He always gave 110 per cent to the things he loved doing, and probably about 10 per cent to the rest!' Look, you can't be good at everything, can you?

I still spent more time talking to the adults on duty in the playground than I did playing with the other kids my own age. I wasn't keen on games or sports; I don't know why. I just preferred the company of

grown-ups, and I always appreciated a captive audience – even back then. I remember spending so much time persuading various teachers to watch me perform my latest magic trick. I probably got on their nerves – except for Miss Gardiner, that is. She was always very encouraging in whatever I was doing, and she always tried to give the kids in her classes room to express themselves. She told my Mum, 'I always enjoyed watching Dan's magic, and I loved his enthusiasm. Seeing that passion ooze out of every orifice! He was so determined. When Dan told you he was going to be famous magician, you absolutely believed him.' She definitely had a lot more patience with me than some of the other teachers!

I was in the Glee Club Miss Gardiner ran for a while. We got to sing at a Young Voices concert at Manchester Arena. Young Voices put on some of the biggest children's choir events, all over the world; there were about 8,000 kids singing, including our school Glee Club, and me!

Yes, where there was entertaining to be done, I was always keen to get involved. Which is why I was also did well in the school talent show three years running – doing magic, of course. And with each year, I felt like I was getting progressively better.

One of my brother Harrison and my favourite things to do when we were kids was to recreate music videos. Well, they weren't so much recreations, more our own dramatic interpretations of the songs. We'd spend all day filming them together: outside locations, cars, running around the house in mad outfits, whatever was required for the scenes, we went for it. When the filming was done, Harrison would edit them for maximum impact. I remember a favourite being 'Fight

For This Love' by Cheryl Cole – that was a pretty decent one. Harrison always had great instincts when it came to getting things down on film; he's one of the main reasons I developed such a love of making videos and I guess that's why he's still in that world now: studying filmmaking at university in Manchester.

I've always been close to my brother, but we think quite differently, which I suppose is a good thing. Harrison is much more chilled and laidback about stuff, while I'm always 'Go! Go! Go!' Where we are the same though, is that we've both always known what we like doing and what we're into. Back then, we both went to an after-school drama club called Starstruck Talent. I think I'd started going there when I was as young as four. Our routine was that we'd get home from school, get changed, and then head off to Starstruck, which was run by two drama teachers.

THE DRAMA CLUB WAS SOMETHING I REALLY STARTED TO CLICK WITH

Mum set up a talent agency that was linked to the drama club. That way, she could look out for auditions and opportunities for kids who attended. The Starstruck Talent Agency did OK for a while; some of the kids did get a few bits and pieces of work out of it, including my brother and me. The trouble was, most of the auditions tended to be in London. A lot of the parents couldn't afford to spend a hundred quid on train fare to get them and their kid to London and back for an audition that was probably a long shot anyway.

Harrison was always more interested in acting than I was – at the beginning it was just a hobby and I didn't take it all that seriously – but as I got a bit older I really started to get into it and understand what acting was all about. By the time I was about seven, with my imagination starting to fly, the drama club was something I really started to click with. While I was there, I felt like I was in my element. It didn't matter what part I had to play; I just loved having a script or lines to concentrate on. I could dive into the role and escape my everyday life. Not that everyday life was all that bad or boring, but you know what I mean.

As kids, we live in our imagination a lot of the time – I did anyway. I'd watch a film or a TV show, or read a book, and imagine myself in the situation and the world I was seeing in front of me. Acting allowed me to be someone else for a while; I could take on any character and become that person. I loved it, and I felt like I was good at it. It became something I wanted to pursue.

After I'd been acting for a while, I landed an audition for a TV advert through the Starstruck agency. I never really thought I'd get it, so I just looked on it as a bit of fun and a day out in London. At the end of the audition, I thanked the casting directors for seeing me and told everyone involved what a fantastic time I'd had. I reckon that's why I got a callback. By being polite and appreciative, I like to think I stuck in their minds. It's something I've done ever since in auditions or in other situations where it might be called for, because I feel like it's essential. Ultimately I got the part.

The advert turned out to be for the fresh-fish counter at Morrisons supermarkets and I played one of a group of kids watching a fishing boat unload their catch at a harbour. I had to take pictures of one of the fish with a plastic camera. You then saw the same kids at the fresh-fish counter in Morrisons, at which point, I held up my camera with my fish photo and asked, 'Have you got this one?' The funny thing was, that line wasn't even in the script. Honestly, it was all so new to me, and I didn't even realise they were filming at that moment. However, everyone on set burst out laughing, so they ended up keeping the line in and ending the advert with it. It's something I've found with my videos and performances over the years; some of the best and funniest moments are the ones you don't plan – the spontaneous, unscripted ones.

I ended up doing a few more TV ads for Morrisons. In 2011 I was in their Christmas adverts with the cricketer Freddie Flintoff and the legend that was Bruce Forsyth – he of the famous catchphrase 'Nice to see you, to see you nice!' – when he was still presenting *Strictly Come Dancing*.

Mum was obviously keen to get us on telly! When I was nine I also appeared with her and my brother on a show called *Turn Back Time, The Family*. This was something Mum had spotted in an advert while she was running the agency. The BBC were looking for families to take

THE EPISODE IS FULL OF SHOTS OF ME PULLING FACES AT HOW DISGUSTING THE FOOD WAS

part in a show where they'd be transported back in time, so to speak! Each family would live for a week exactly as they would have in a past decade, only having access to the things that were around back then.

It was a filmed experiment, exploring life for families in various eras from the past, and they covered periods as far back as the Victorians. Our episode didn't go that far back, thank God, but it was still a big learning curve, especially for my brother and me. Our episode was all about the 1970s, which was the decade when my mum was born.

We moved onto a street where we didn't know anyone – Mum was worrying about how nice the neighbours were going to be – with a TV crew following our every move. Mum could remember some things from being a kid, but only really knew what Gran had told her about those days. Meanwhile, my brother Harrison and I didn't have a clue what to expect!

While filming a TV show was a fun experience, the fact that we ended up living in a fairly basic home, with no technology, games, toys or phones, made me appreciate everything I had in the twenty-first century. The episode focused on how difficult it was for single mums back then, bringing up kids on their own with little money. There certainly weren't any of the luxuries we were used to, oh no! In fact, we didn't even have a proper oven. It was just this tiny, crappy looking thing called a Baby Belling. It was the sort of thing you might take on a camping trip – it looked ancient! To be honest, the whole place just looked horrible, old and drab.

'It's not very nice, I don't really like it,' said a young sad-faced me to the camera. 'It's a bit tacky and there's not much to do!'

Tacky!? Wow! I was obviously quite selective about my surroundings, even back then! Even Mum described some of the household stuff there as minging, and spent half her time wiping everything down, wishing she could just chuck it away instead.

While we were there, Mum cooked us typical 1970s food on the antique cooking whatnot: budget sausages, instant mash and these weird-looking tinned peas, which I hated. Actually, the episode is full of shots of me pulling faces at how disgusting the food was. I was not in the least impressed.

From what I learned about the 1970s, Mum would have been going out to work every week day, yet only have about a pound a day to live on after rent and all the bills were paid. That seems unbelievable

DAVID COPPERFIELD

The image I'll never forget of David Copperfield is the one of him floating over the Grand Canyon while Bonnie Tyler sings 'Holding Out For A Hero'. Very retro-1980s – but then again, I do love my 1980s music! It's not the sort of magic I'd attempt, but I think it was perfect for that era, when everything was big and bold! Stuff he's done like making the Statue of Liberty disappear or the Grand Canyon illusion is just timeless magic. Brilliant entertainment.

Like me, David started young. When he was ten, he started performing magic in his local area, under the name 'Davino the Boy Magician'. By the time he was twelve, he was the youngest person to be admitted to the Society of American Magicians.

David has been recognised as the most commercially successful magician in history. His TV specials have won 21 Emmy Awards over the years, and tickets sales to his shows have grossed over $4 billion. I mean, the man's an actual legend!

It's not always been plain sailing, though. In 1984, during rehearsals for an illusion where he was chained up in a tank of water, he got tangled in the chains and started taking in water, ending up being rushed to hospital. I'll stick with the playing cards, thanks!

One of my earliest memories of watching magic on YouTube was seeing a video of him from way back in the 1980s when he makes a playing card go through the window of a moving train. I actually learned how to do that trick myself and still do it now.

now! This was mainly because women's wages were so terrible back then, and there was nowhere near the same opportunities for women as there were for men. Plus, that one pound had to go for food, clothes and everything else we might need as a family.

To make the whole thing even more realistic, we had a power cut while we were there and the water was turned off so we couldn't even flush the toilet. Then there was a dustmen's strike, so there were stinking rubbish bags piling up outside the house. Apparently, this was what many people had to put up with back in the day. Lovely! I remember thinking, thank God I wasn't really around back in the 1970s. It was proper grim!

I COULDN'T GET ENOUGH OF SEEING HIM DO THIS AMAZING TRICK

My diversion into acting was a lot of fun, but even then, my passion for magic still burned bright. When I was filming one of the Morrisons adverts, I met a guy who showed me an illusion where he levitated. How did he do that? Every time I saw him on location, I begged him to show me again. I couldn't get enough of seeing him do this amazing trick.

Once after he did it for me, he told me, 'On a good day, I can get much higher.' Flying was something I'd watched the brilliant American illusionist David Copperfield do on one of his old TV shows, but it blew me away seeing it happen in front of my eyes. I remember saying to him, 'What are you doing with a job like this when you can fly?'

Eventually, the man was kind enough to show me the secret of levitation for myself. In fact, I ended doing it in one of my very first videos and I've shared the secret with you too!

THE FIRST MAGICIANS

The art of magic goes back to the time of the ancient Egyptians, but back then it didn't come in the form of card tricks and rabbits in hats. (Actually, I'm not sure a rabbit would even have fitted in those hats!) There's an ancient Egyptian text that tells of a man called Dedi who amazed the pharaohs with his sorcery. It was said that Dedi was 110 years old, could eat 500 loaves of bread and drink 100 pints of beer every day. Unsurprisingly, there's no actual evidence that he ever really existed. Real or not, Dedi is still remembered for his ability to bring birds back to life. I know! Apparently, he'd cut their heads off and then re-attacheded them. Of course, at the time, this was thought to be the work of the gods. If he really did exist, I reckon he'd mastered a pretty impressive illusion.

Fast forward to Roman times, a time when, historians believe, magic started to be used as entertainment rather than just for witchcraft and sorcery. The first real evidence of magic as showmanship are accounts of performances of the cups-and-balls trick. It's now world famous, but the first people to do the trick were a band of Roman magicians known as the Acetabularii, who used small cups and stones to perform it. I think we can safely say that this was the very first recorded sleight-of-hand magic trick.

The word 'sleight' comes from an old Norse word that translates as something like 'quick fingers' or 'trickster fingers'. That's pretty much on the nose as a description goes. Over the centuries, magicians have often used it in close-up magic, the kind of settings where the audience can really see their movements. Of course, the trick is, while the audience is concentrating on one thing, there's always something else going on that they don't see. It's basically deception!

As well as the cup-and-balls trick, there's also some evidence of disappearing tricks used to entertain in Roman times. After that, not much is known about how magic developed, only that it was frowned upon and was unpopular in many cultures for a very long time. Not any more though, I'm pleased to say!

DECK OF CARDS

OK, so my favourite tool when it comes to magic is and always has been a deck of cards. Simple, classic, perfect!

A HANDFUL OF POSSIBILITIES

So, why do I love them so much? Well, apart from anything else, there's so much you can do with them. In fact, the possibilities are endless.

There's a lot of history behind the humble deck of cards. I always think it's like holding a piece of history in your hand, and that's why I love performing with them.

52 CARDS IN A DECK

A deck of cards represents a full calendar year – and all the infinite possibilities that could happen as a year goes by.

Why? Well, there are 52 cards in a deck, which represent the number of weeks in a year. There are four suits – hearts, spades, clubs and diamonds – the four seasons. And all the pips in a deck of cards add up to 365, the number of days in a year. Amazing! Also, every time you shuffle a deck of cards, it will land in a unique order that it's never been in before and will never be in again. Think about that!

THE VANISHING GLASS

The great thing about this trick is that the audience's expectations start off low, just thinking that you're going make a coin disappear, but then it turns into something completely different.

What you'll need: Believe it or not . . . a glass! Also, a coin and some tin foil. And a table.

1 Place the coin on the table between you and the audience and put the glass upside down over the coin. Cover the glass completely with the tin foil and tell everyone that you're about to make the coin disappear.

2 Snap your fingers and lift the glass – the coin is still there! Repeat this a few times so it seems like the trick isn't working.

turn over

3 While the audience is concentrating on the coin, sneakily pull the glass out of the tin foil and put it in your lap, using the table as cover — the tin foil will keep its glass-like shape.

4 Place the hollow tin foil back over the coin, so it looks like the glass is still over it.

5 Count down – 3,2,1, then slam your hand down on the tin foil, squashing it flat. Once you've got the hang of this you could even finish with a final flourish, by revealing the glass from your lap so it appears as if it's gone straight through the table!

what?!

THROWING A CARD

This is something I've always done with cards, and it's so much fun. All you need is some cards . . . and maybe something to throw them at!

1 Grip a card between your index and middle finger.

If you work on your aim, you can hit things right across a room. Don't throw them at anyone. I once threw a card at my mum. It didn't end well.

2 Tilt your wrist back.

3 Then flick it forward, letting go of the card as your fingers point outward.

THE LEVITATING CARD

Lifting a card – making it look like it's levitating out of the pack – is a simple but effective trick.

Gently grip the pack of cards between your thumb and hand, then rest the index finger of your other hand on top of the pack while pushing your pinkie finger firmly against the back of the pack.

As you raise your index finger slide the back card up with your pinkie! Simple, right?

THE *BEST* WAY TO PREDICT
THE FUTURE IS TO

CREATE IT

THE YOUNG PERFORMER

One thing I enjoyed when I was young was my regular trip to a close-up magicians' group that met in Manchester every month. It's funny, when I first started doing magic, I had this strange idea that I was the only person my age who was into it. There was certainly no one else at my primary school doing it, and none of my friends outside school were into it either. Turning up for the first time at the magicians' circle changed all that. It was a great feeling to realise that there were other nerds my age who were as obsessed with magic as I was.

The best things about it were seeing the same faces every month and the fact we were all there for a shared goal: to learn about and discuss magic. The event would start off with one of the adult magicians performing a trick, followed by a demonstration of how it was done. After that, it turned into more of a social vibe, with everyone just hanging out and showing off various tricks. I actually made a lot of friends at the monthly magic circle.

You won't be surprised to hear that, by then, I'd turned into a proper little performer as far as magic was concerned. I wasn't exactly shy anymore! It was like, if I saw a group of people gathered anywhere, then I saw it as my duty to go and spread some happiness and magic among them. I'd wander up to random people and perform tricks for them wherever I went. I was somehow compelled to entertain. I remember, being at an Indian restaurant one New Year's Eve, and going around doing tricks for all the guests. I don't recall being at all nervous back then; I was just being a giddy kid showing off what I could do.

I DON'T RECALL BEING AT ALL NERVOUS BACK THEN

My impromptu performance at the restaurant led to someone there asking if I would do some magic at their upcoming wedding. Then, at the wedding, another guest asked me perform at another event. It just went on from there.

Mind you, it took me a while to get the performance side of things right. At one big charity event, a guy called me over and asked if I'd try a trick out for him and the people on his table.

TO THIS DAY, IT WAS THE EASIEST TWENTY POUNDS I'VE EVER MADE

'If you can make one card change for another in my hand, I'll give you twenty pounds.'

Well, I love a challenge, and I could do that with no trouble. So, the guy chose a card – three of hearts – and I put it in his hand. He closed his hand, then opened it again, looking back at the card. King of spades!

'I really didn't believe you could do that,' he said. 'That's amazing!'

To this day, it was the easiest twenty pounds I've ever made!

As well as walking away from the table a richer man, I also had an idea. Straight after, I went over to a guy at another table, telling him that, for twenty pounds, I could make a card change from one to another in his hand without him noticing. I'm not sure if it was because I was cute, persuasive or just that he didn't want to say no to an eight-year-old kid, but he agreed. A few minutes later, I was walking away with another crisp twenty-pound note. Now this was getting pretty good.

It was at that moment that it dawned on me that magic might not just be something I did for fun; it was also a way of making money. True, I might have been a little bit young to be worrying about how I was going to make my fortune, but the idea of performing magic tricks at parties and events for money was a good one. That night seemed as good a time to start as any. So, for the rest of the evening, I made my way around the tables, smiling sweetly and offering to do the trick for twenty pounds – and I found that most of the guests were up for it. At the end of the night, I had a grand. That's right – £1000! I'd managed to get to around fifty people that night.

The problem was, I'd got a bit carried away as the night went on. Rather than asking if people wanted to see the trick, I'd just told them, 'Pull out twenty quid, I've got something to show you!' Then I'd grab the cash, do the trick and walk off. Most people laughed, but one man complained to the organisers that I'd robbed twenty quid off him. Can you imagine? There was a bit of a commotion and it ended up with me having to give a couple of people their money back. Maybe I wasn't quite as ready to be a paid entertainer as I thought.

As it turned out, though, most of the guests loved my cheekiness and went away highly entertained and twenty quid poorer. Of course, we gave the whole lot to the charity in the end! I expect that was probably my mum's idea. Although I kept a small percentage to buy some new magic tricks – but don't tell anyone!

As I fell into bed that night, I felt like there might actually be a future in becoming a professional magician. I was just going to have to make a few minor adjustments to my act – maybe learn to read the room a bit more carefully!

Not long after I got my chance: a post-match event at Oldham Athletic Football Club, when I was about nine. Mum had been invited through her work, and it was a 'bring your kids'-type invitation, so she'd brought her kids! Right, so there I was, making the rounds and showing tricks to anyone who'd give me the time of a day, when one of the guys who was running the event approached my mum.

'Would it be OK if I took your son to perform some tricks for some of our VIPs?' he asked her. 'I think they'd really get a kick out of it.'

I was standing next to my mum, nodding my head like mad, like I'd already decided I was going.

'Yeah, of course you can,' Mum said, so off I went, excitedly trotting along behind this bloke as he led me to another section of the room.

The next thing I knew, I was performing to some of the Oldham players and their VIP guests. There were also players and VIPs from Preston North End, who were the side Oldham had played that day.

It's funny, but I could tell by the reactions of people that I was doing something good, something they were genuinely enjoying. I liked that feeling; the feeling that I was doing something I loved, but that other people were also buying into it. I guess I must have been a hit, because somebody from the Preston North End side asked if they could book me to come and perform at one of their club events too.

That turned out not to be quite as straight-forward as it first sounded. If you take on a professional magic engagement, you can't just turn up and start doing tricks. You have to have a licence, which was something my mum had to sort out fast so I could do the gig! Still, as you can imagine, I was over the moon at the idea of this, especially as it was to be my first professional gig! That's right, I was going to get paid for something I would have happily done for free.

To be honest, I couldn't for the life of me tell you who any of the players or the VIPs were at the post-match events I performed at; I've never really been into football in a big way. Still, I could tell they looked important, and let's face it, an audience is an audience, right?

I was at the now-famous match in 2013, where Oldham beat Liverpool 3–2 in the fourth round of the FA Cup.

> *I WAS GOING TO GET PAID FOR SOMETHING I WOULD HAVE HAPPILY DONE FOR FREE*

I remember that day being really exciting; getting swept up in the crowd as we all ran onto the pitch. It was a good feeling to know that my hometown club had beaten one of the country's very best teams, even though I wasn't the biggest football fan.

It was around that time that I met Gareth Oliver for the third time, when we went to see him in panto. By then, I was pretty skilled as far as magic tricks went. After the show, I was able to show him a few nifty card tricks of my own, and he could see how much I'd learned.

'Wow, Dan! You've gone well above my level now,' he said. It meant a lot coming from one of the first people to show me their tricks, especially as seeing somebody making a living from their act had given me that first little spark of what I wanted to do. I remember feeling very proud of myself. The student had overtaken the master. How cool was that?

It's weird to think that, by the time I was nine years old, I was an actual professional magician – performing at various events and getting paid for doing something I loved.

By then, everything was about magic, and showing off my skills to as many people as I possibly could. I suppose that's why I first auditioned for *Britain's Got Talent*, in December 2012. I remember lining up with hundreds of other people for what felt like an eternity, all of us hoping to get a slot on the live show. Of course, my mum came with me, but to be honest, she hadn't been all that keen on me going up for it. She felt that it wasn't necessarily the best platform for a nine-year-old magician. I could see what she meant. Back then, I hadn't seen any young magicians on *BGT* either. I think Mum was worried that I might get lost in among all the other unsuccessful performers, the

BY THE TIME I WAS NINE YEARS OLD, I WAS AN ACTUAL PROFESSIONAL MAGICIAN

ones who appear on the show but are then never heard of again. Still, I really wanted to have a crack at it, so in the end, I'd managed to persuade her that I should at least give it a try.

Things actually went pretty well that first time. I did some card tricks for a couple of the show's producers and then next thing I knew I'd been whisked away to chat to the researchers, do a bit more filming, and meet some more producers. At the end of the day, they asked Mum if they could send a camera crew to our house to film me waking up in the morning and getting ready, as if it was the day of my live audition – which they did.

'It's looking good,' Mum admitted. I'll be honest, I felt quite excited.

I dropped someone's thirty-grand engagement ring!

Still, Christmas came and went, but the callback for an audition in front of the judges never came. I was gutted, but there was always next year. And If I couldn't perform for Simon Cowell and the *BGT* judges, there were plenty of other people around to show off my skills to! So, we move on . . .

Of course, things don't always go to plan in life, and I've had my share of crazy moments when tricks go wrong or take an unexpected turn.

Back then, I used to do this one trick called The Lifting Trick, where you get someone to lift you up (I was a lot smaller then) but there suddenly comes a point when you literally won't budge and they can't lift you any further. I remember, at one event, this guy got so frustrated that he couldn't get me any further off the ground, he left actual bruises on my body where he'd squeezed so tightly. That was a painful lesson!

I'VE HAD MY SHARE OF CRAZY MOMENTS WHEN TRICKS GO WRONG

Then there was the Disappearing Ring Trick – which twice caused me problems. The idea was that I took a ring off someone, made it disappear, then make it reappear inside a wallet in a sealed envelope. Well, the first time I tried it, I dropped someone's thirty-grand engagement ring. It literally bounced across the floor of a hall, out of sight. The look of horror on everyone's faces was unbelievable, and for a few seconds, you could have heard a pin drop – or in this case, a ring! Suddenly, everyone was crawling round on the floor trying to find it – I was so embarrassed.

A month or so later, I tried the same trick on another young woman, with more success. Well, I say success . . . This time, the ring did actually end up in a sealed envelope inside the wallet as planned. In fact, the trick was so convincing, the woman refused to believe that the ring inside the envelope was actually her ring at all. She thought I'd swapped her ring for a fake one. She just didn't believe any of it was possible.

I sort of brushed it off at first, thinking she might get over it, but a little while later, her husband came over and pulled me to one side.

'Look, is there any chance you could show her how the trick works, because she's genuinely upset.'

Sure enough, she was in the toilets, crying, convinced that she'd lost her ring forever. The only way I could convince her that I wasn't some sophisticated child jewel thief was to take her through the magic trick stage by stage; show her exactly what I'd done and how it worked. The power of magic, eh?

On the other hand, sometimes things happen that are just pure fluke. Like the time I thought I'd hypnotised someone.

This was at a New Year's Eve party when I was about eleven. I persuaded a guy I didn't know to let me practise my technique and have a go at hypnotising him. He agreed, and off I went, going through my well-rehearsed script while he sat there on a chair in front of me.

Eventually, when I gave the command, 'Sleep', the guy slipped off the chair onto the floor. I could hardly believe what had happened, but I kept going.

'Stand up,' I said. 'Now do twenty press-ups. Now dance back and forth. Now bark like a dog.'

He did it all, every mad thing I told him to do, much to the delight of the other guests. I even made the poor guy forget his name at one

I hypnotised someone!

DERREN BROWN

Derren Brown is a mentalist, which a different kind of magic altogether – one that I find fascinating.

He grew up not far from London, and actually studied law at university before getting into performing close-up magic in bars and restaurants. Eventually, he became more of a psychological illusionist, but he doesn't claim to have any psychic powers. Actually some of his performances expose methods of people who *do* claim to have supernatural powers. As Derren Brown explains, he actually uses a blend of hypnosis, illusion, the power of suggestion, and good old-fashioned showmanship.

Over the years, he's had loads of TV series and specials, and some of them proved quite controversial with audiences – with titles like *Heist* and *Russian Roulette*, I suppose that's not surprising. He's also performed a fair amount of stage tours, packing out theatres with his award-winning live shows, which is also something I'd love to do.

Like most of my other heroes, I've watched a lot of his work on YouTube. I think I admired him mainly because his brand of magic is so very different from other illusionists and magicians – he works with the mind rather than the eye. His ability to hypnotise and manipulate people, persuading them to do crazy, ridiculous stuff, sometimes making complete idiots of themselves in front of a massive live audience, intrigues me.

The other thing is, I always somehow feel smarter after watching Derren Brown; there's so much stuff about psychology and the inner workings of the brain involved. I always feel like I've learned something new after seeing one of his videos.

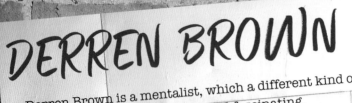

point. I felt like I had a new superpower. Looking back, I can't be sure if the prank was actually on me and that he was just going along with it for a laugh. Still, it all looked pretty convincing at the time; he seemed like he was hypnotised and acting under my control. I was on top of the world that night. Not only was I a professional magician, but I was now a hypnotist. I was moving up in the world.

The next day, I tried my skill out on someone else, but to my utter disappointment, it completely failed. I thought I must have lost my touch. That superpower didn't last long, did it? Since then, I've managed to do it a few times over the years, mostly on kids at school. It seems to work on some people but not others. I guess it all depends on what kind of mind you have and how susceptible you are to the power of suggestion.

A few years later, the guy I'd hypnotised at the New Year's Eve party called me out of the blue, having found one of the business cards I'd handed out that night in an old wallet. 'Hey, mate, how are you?' he said. 'I'm finally getting married, and I wondered if you'd like to come and do some magic at our wedding reception?' If he'd remembered me after all that time, he was clearly impressed by whatever I'd done that night. So perhaps I really had hypnotised him after all!

Talking of flukes, I once told a girl I could read minds but she wasn't convinced. 'Right, what number am I thinking of?' she fired back.

'Thirty-five,' I said, picking a random number out of thin air.

The girls jaw dropped. 'That was my number,' she said.

'There you go.' I'd even surprised myself.

And speaking of reading minds, dear reader, I'd like you to think of a number between one and ten right now – only not the number three – the first one that pops into your mind. Have you got it? Perfect! Then I want you think of a random vegetable – the first that comes to mind. Got it? Good! Then finally, think of a tool. Again, the first one that pops into your mind. OK? Great! Now turn the page . . .

You were thinking of the number seven, a carrot and a hammer. How many did I get right? LOL!

It's weird, but our minds tend to organise information in a certain way. There are loads of different vegetables, and you'd probably be able to name a lot of them. The thing is, when you're asked to name just one as quickly as possible, the most obvious vegetable you can think of is often a carrot! It's what science calls a 'prototypical' idea of what a vegetable is. It's the same with cards. If you ask someone to pick a playing card, the most popular go-to for the brain is the Queen of Hearts. That's not just magic, it's science!

SOMETIMES, IT'S THE TRICKS THAT ARE THE SIMPLEST AND EASIEST TO UNDERSTAND THAT ARE THE MOST POWERFUL

In those early days, I got my magic fix from watching YouTube videos, which is why that platform has always been so important to me. It's how I consumed content as a kid and how I learned about magic. The majority of the stuff I was learning back then involved cards. They were most definitely the rabbit holes I went down as far as YouTube went. That was how I learned one of my favourite tricks, the one where you put one card in somebody's hand and change it to another. The trick that I'd earned all that money from at the charity event. It's so simple, but the reactions I've got from people witnessing something completely change right there in their hand are some of the best. In life, you often hear the phrase 'less is more', and I think that's

DAVID BLAINE

David Blaine is an American illusionist, best known as an endurance artist and extreme performer. He was one of the first magicians I came across on YouTube, and what I noticed when I watched his street-magic videos was that he didn't look like a magician – at least not like I imagined a magician to look. There was no cape, no hat and no wand, which I could identify with, being just an ordinary kid obsessed with magic.

Over the years, he's put himself through all sorts in the name of entertainment, going to great lengths to master his skills. He once said his favourite performer was Hadji Ali, whose most spectacular stunt was to swallow lots of water followed by a bottle of kerosene, then spout the kerosene out from his stomach over a flame, followed by the water, which put the flame out. In the end, that trick actually killed Hadji, but David Blaine was obsessed with figuring out how he did it, and eventually mastered it himself.

Some of his own crazier feats have included being submerged in a sphere of liquid for seven days, suspended in a box dangling over the River Thames in London with no food, only water, for 44 days, and being frozen in a block of ice in the middle of Times Square in New York for 72 hours.

His most recent stunt was in 2020 when he floated 20,000 feet into the sky holding on to 52 helium-filled balloons, before leaving go and parachuting back down.

My favourite video, though, is of him levitating in front of different groups of people. It's just incredible seeing his feet literally lift off the ground. Of course, I had to learn to do that one myself!

very often the case. Sometimes, it's the tricks that are the simplest and easiest to understand that are the most powerful.

Actually, for anyone reading this wanting to learn some brilliant card tricks (I should imagine that's quite a few of you), I can highly recommend a YouTube channel called The Card Trick Teacher – there are so many incredible tricks on there. There were other channels I loved when I started too: Disturbed Reality was a channel that taught cool magic tricks, and 52 Kards was another.

Given how much time I spent watching videos on YouTube, one of my friends encouraged me to make a video of my own. YouTube was the first place I wanted my magic to be seen and so that was where I started my channel. My first video was called 'Dan, Dan, The Magic Man'. It was a clip of me introducing myself, aged nine, talking about my love of Dynamo, and showing off my skills with a deck of cards around the estate where I lived. This was one of my first times performing the trick where you ask someone to write their name on a card, then make the card appear on the inside of a nearby car window. A lot of people first saw the card-in-car-window trick when another of my heroes, David Blaine, did it in a car advert back in the 1990s. I also levitated live on camera! OK, it wasn't as slick as some of my later efforts, but it was a start!

In another early video, I made a card float out of the pack for my Granny Margaret, but unfortunately, the video got zero views. Nothing. Yes, I was disappointed, but I wasn't going to give up yet.

I couldn't have imagined then how much my channel would grow over the years and what an important role the internet and social media would play in my life. It's funny to think that I started my magic career by watching all these YouTubers perform, and now here I am, doing it myself.

THE MENTALISTS

A mentalist is a physic performer who possesses highly developed mental skills. They perform crazy acts of the mind that can trick their audience into believing that they actually have these other-worldly supernatural powers.

Some historians believe that certain mentalists may have used their powers to influence the course of history. It's said that both Adolf Hitler and Joseph Stalin were influenced by the clever techniques of psychic performers who they took into their confidence. But it goes back even further than that!

Back in days of old, fortune tellers and prophets were considered gods. The Ancient Greeks and Romans treated every prophecy like it was a direct message from above. Still, while all these blokes in togas actually believed they were getting tips and messages from the gods, most

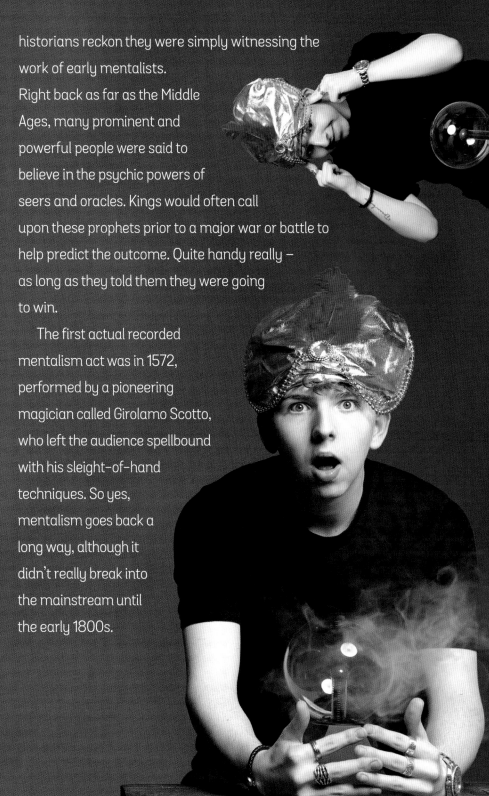

historians reckon they were simply witnessing the work of early mentalists.

Right back as far as the Middle Ages, many prominent and powerful people were said to believe in the psychic powers of seers and oracles. Kings would often call upon these prophets prior to a major war or battle to help predict the outcome. Quite handy really – as long as they told them they were going to win.

The first actual recorded mentalism act was in 1572, performed by a pioneering magician called Girolamo Scotto, who left the audience spellbound with his sleight-of-hand techniques. So yes, mentalism goes back a long way, although it didn't really break into the mainstream until the early 1800s.

THE CRAZY ACES

This is the trick that my dad's friend, Uncle Ste taught me and is one of the earliest card tricks I learnt.

What you'll need: One deck of cards.

shhh!!

1 Out of sight, spread out the cards to find the four aces, then put all four aces on the top of the deck, face down.

2 Hand the deck to your participant and instruct them to deal four cards from the top of the deck, putting them face down in a pile (these will be the aces so it's very important they're face down!).

Make sure they've dealt the four aces before you say they can deal from anywhere in the deck!

3 Then, after they have dealt the four aces face down, they can carry on dealing on to the pile from wherever they want in the deck, stopping whenever they want.

turn over

4 When they've finished, ask them to pick up their pile and deal the cards face down from the top, this time dividing them into four separate piles.

5 Once all their cards are dealt into four piles, challenge them to turn over the top card of each pile. These four cards will be the four aces!

KEY CARD

Although this is quite simple to do, it relies on you being able to subconsciously influence your participant to put their card on the pile you want them to.

What you'll need: One deck of cards.

1 While no one is looking have a sneaky peak at the top card in the deck, you need to remember this as it is your 'key card'. Once you've got that memorised, fan the full deck out and ask your participant to select a card from the deck and look at it, without showing you what it is.

2 Then divide the deck into two piles (making sure your key card is on the top of one of the piles) and ask your participant to put their card on top of one of the piles. This is the tricky bit as you need to make sure their card ends up on top of your key card but without saying anything.

3 Now pick up both piles and put them on top of one another, making sure the pile they put their card on is underneath the other one.

4 Then spread all the cards out on the table and look for your key card. If your subtle powers of persuasion have worked then whatever card is the next in line after your key card is the card they chose.

SNAP CHANGE

This is a difficult one to master, but worth the time – especially if you're an eight-year-old kid looking to make a quick twenty pounds!

What you'll need:
One deck of cards.
A lot of practice!

shhh!!

1 You need two cards in your hand, but pushed tight one behind the other, so it looks like you're just holding one card.

2 Place your first and second finger on the bottom corner of the card, with your thumb resting on the back of the cards.

3 Snap your finger, so you're pushing the card that was at the top to the back, making it look like the card has changed, just like magic!.

Practise until you can do it REALLY fast!

NEVER FORGET THAT

LESS IS MORE

THE CHOCOLATE FACTORY

Throughout primary school, I kept going to Starstruck and also got involved with anything to do with acting at school. You could say that being in the limelight was something I'd taken to naturally. I thoroughly enjoyed being on stage, but I especially loved musical theatre.

The primary teacher I mentioned, Miss Gardiner, was in charge of casting the school productions, and she always gave me a part. I made sure I was very dedicated when it came to studying and learning for a role. True, I might not have been the most academic of students, but I could learn and memorise a script, no problem.

> SHE SAID I HAD THE VOICE OF AN ANGEL – CAN YOU IMAGINE?

When I was nine, she cast me in *The Wizard Of Oz* . . . as the Gatekeeper. OK, so it wasn't a major role, like the Scarecrow or the Tin Man but you've got to start somewhere. It's kind of ironic that I didn't get to play the Wizard himself, given that I'm now a real-life wizard (at least I like to think I am) but the Gatekeeper had more lines than the Wizard anyway so I'll try not to sound bitter! Miss Gardiner told me I really made the part my own. I think what she meant by that was that I added a few bits in, just to make the part bigger than it actually was.

A year later, I managed to bag a bigger role – the starring role, in fact! Having always been a massive fan of *A Christmas Carol*, I was very happy to be playing the part of Scrooge in the school's Christmas production. My voice hadn't broken yet, so Miss Gardiner decided to give me the most ridiculously high song to sing. She said I had the voice of an angel – can you imagine? Mind you, not everyone agreed. I was practically banned from practising my singing at home most of the time. That was mainly because I got on my mum and brother's nerves. They described my so-called angelic singing as 'screeching'. Nice. Thank you, Mum. And I love you too, Bro!

Still, I wasn't deterred. Actually, this was about the time when I seriously got the acting bug, and decided I wanted to take it a bit further. I was even prepared to put magic on the back burner for a bit – can you believe that?

My really big acting break came when I auditioned for the West End production of the musical *Charlie and the Chocolate Factory*, for the part of Mike Teavee, the Golden Ticket-winner who is obsessed with TV – or in this version, video games – and toy pistols.

I WAS SURE I WAS OUT OF MY DEPTH AND THAT I DIDN'T HAVE A HOPE

When I arrived at the London audition, I was overwhelmed by how many other kids there were, desperate to land the role. I think there was about five hundred due to come through the doors that day – kids from Liverpool, Ireland, Wales, Scotland, and, of course, one particular young hopeful from Manchester. Me!

I remember thinking, 'I am never going to get this role. It's not going to happen.' There just seemed to be so much talent surrounding me. At one point, I was sitting there, waiting for my turn, watching one of the other boys practising his audition song, all prepared. Now, I'm not the best singer in the world, so when I heard this kid with his incredible voice, I was sure I was out of my depth and that I didn't have a hope in hell of even getting a callback.

By the time I went into my audition, I'd already been in the building waiting for about two hours.

'We need you to play an angry kid,' the casting director said.

Like most kids, I'd had enough experience of that to give it a go, so off I went.

'Imagine your mum has grounded you, you're not allowed to go out, and you're really unhappy about it.'

Perfect, I thought, I just need to be myself.

Anyway, I did my best angry kid, followed by a bit of singing and some dancing, and before I knew it, it was all over.

The audition process was pretty drawn out over the next few weeks. There were well over a hundred kids at the first callback, then it was cut down and down again. Finally, there were just ten of us at the final callback, and we all knew that only four of us would get the job. They needed four Mike Teavees, because until you're eighteen, the law says you can only work a certain number of days and do a certain number of shows. After that last audition, I must admit I didn't think I'd got it. For weeks we didn't hear anything, so I'd practically given up on it. Then, one afternoon, I got home from school, and my mum and brother started singing 'Pure Imagination', one of the famous songs from the show.

'Dan, you've got the role!'

'WHAT?!!'

I went off, running around the house like crazy, jumping up and down. I was absolutely over the moon; it was an incredible feeling. It was quite a celebration in our house that day.

I'd be thrown into this whole new world of working as a professional actor in a West End show, living away from home, with none of my family around me, in the centre of London. Straight into the deep end. On the very first day of rehearsal, I realised how disciplined I was going to have to be. The director and creative team were pretty strict and to the point. I was there to do a job, and that was that. There was no time for messing about. Of course, other kids in the cast were my age, but I remember being very nervous and shy, not speaking to them very much on that first day. What I didn't know then was that I'd end up living in a flat with some of those other kids for the next year.

One of my most vivid memories is walking into the theatre and seeing the show's set for the very first time. It took my breath away. I was genuinely speechless. I think, at the time, it was the biggest set in the West End, and walking into the auditorium felt almost like the scene in the movie when all the kids first walk into the chocolate room. Totally magical.

The cast rehearsed for about three months before we were ready, but about a week before I was due to go on for my debut performance, something out of the blue happened that shook everything up. At the end of my final week of rehearsals, Mum came down from Manchester with a friend, so we could all have a day out in London together. During that day, we decided to pass by the theatre, just to say hi to everyone. That was when we bumped into Ramona, one of the child chaperones.

'Oh, thank God you got the calls!' she said, sounding relieved.

'What calls?' Mum said.

'We've been trying to get hold of you,' Ramona said. 'Dylan, who's due to go on as Mike Teavee tonight, has been taken ill at school. The team thought, as you were nearby, you could go on in his place.'

'What, a whole week early?

'Yeah,' Romana said. 'They want you to go on tonight.'

It was a shock but to be honest by then I was so ready to go. So, of course, I told the team I would do it. In the end, it was probably much

I have my debut on the West End stage!

better that way as I didn't have time to have a build-up of first-night nerves! Mind you, my heart was still racing just before I made my entrance. When the curtain went down at the end of the show, I felt such a rush having done it. The rest of the cast applauded me and called out, 'Let's go, Dan! That was great!' It was such a good feeling to have that all-important first performance done and dusted, even though it was by complete fluke. A week later, my entire family came down, all excited to see me in my debut performance. But I had to come clean after the show and admit that it actually wasn't at all.

WE LIVED AND WORKED TOGETHER THE WHOLE TIME, ALL GOING THROUGH THIS BRILLIANT SHARED EXPERIENCE

The show was at the Theatre Royal, in Drury Lane in London. Home in Shaw was more than two hundred miles away. While the show was on, I lived in London with a chaperone and three of the other actors. Like me, these were kids who lived too far away to go back and forth to their homes each night. Amy was from Huddersfield in Yorkshire, Vincent was from Kent, and Rhys, who played Charlie, was Scottish. I'd be there for two weeks, doing eight shows a week, and then I'd have a week off, back home. It might sound like a cliché, but Amy, Vincent and Charlie, and our chaperones, became like family to me because we lived and worked together the whole time, all going through this brilliant shared experience.

There was a hell of a lot to fit into every two weeks of work. Just because I was working didn't mean I could miss school and forget about my studies (no such luck!). Every night, when the curtain came down, we'd run off stage, get out of our costumes and wigs, and then head back to the flat, which was just outside Covent Garden, not too far from the theatre. By the time we got home and to bed, it was half past eleven. In the morning we'd have to be up again at six to get showered and dressed for our tutoring sessions, which started at seven o'clock at the theatre.

While I was working on *Charlie and the Chocolate Factory*, pranks were a big thing between the younger cast members. As I'm sure you can imagine, I was right up there at the forefront when it came to instigating them. I loved it.

Poor Rhys – the kid who played Charlie in the show – bore the brunt of one of my earliest and most elaborate pranks while we were living together in the flat. It was a crazy idea, really. I'm not sure how or why I thought of it, or what compelled me to do it. But hey, I did it!

A few nights after we'd settled in, I told Rhys that I wasn't merely a magician but an actual magical being. An angel. I went on to explain that I wasn't a living person at all and that I had appeared only in his imagination to offer him guidance and sage life advice. OK, so Rhys might have been young and inexperienced in the ways of magic, but he wasn't silly. Of course, his reaction was something along the lines of, 'Yeah, Dan, OK! Whatever!' Just as you'd expect. Still, that was the seed of my plan. And however disbelieving Rhys was, I'd well-and-truly planted it!

That same evening, I took a photo of Rhys and me together on my iPad. After printing it off and handing it to him as a gift, I then went back to the image on the iPad and used an app to edit me out of it completely. You can see where I'm going with this, right?

Now, you can't pull off a plan like this without the assistance of others, so I convinced everyone in the apartment to play along with

I made someone think I'd disappeared!

NERVES CAN BE A GOOD THING!

To me, nerves are a good thing for being a performer. You might not think it, but it can be a great asset when you channel those nerves and that adrenaline in the right way. I can never quite get my head around people who say they never suffer from nerves before they're about to perform. If you're nervous, it means that you care about what you're about to do.

Nerves are nothing more than an adrenaline rush.

The best thing to do with nerves or fear is to acknowledge that you're feeling it and then channel that feeling into being the best you can possibly be. Accept that you're going to be nervous because what you're doing is important to you, and then just go for it! Try not to overthink it; embrace it and have fun.

Nervousness can show up in many different ways: shaky hands, dry mouth, sweating, heart racing, or even your mind going totally blank. Any of them have the potential to cause problems if you're about to perform. And if you get two or three of them at the same time you could really be in trouble. My advice: take deep breaths and try to calm your mind.

These days, I tell myself I'm not nervous, I'm excited. It's a good way of turning it on its head!

the prank. I even convinced Deborah, one of the chaperones, to get in on it, genuinely believing that it was all a bit of harmless fun.

Early the next day, I packed every bit of my stuff into a suitcase and hid it under the bed in Deborah's room, where we weren't allowed to go. After that, I printed off the edited picture and swapped it with the original I'd given to Rhys. Then I got under the bed with the suitcase. All evidence of me ever being in the flat had vanished.

I was stuck under that bed for over an hour before Rhys woke up, but when he did, I was just about able to hear what was happening on the other side of the door.

'Where's Dan?' I heard him ask.

'I'm sorry?' Deborah said.

'Dan, where is he?'

'Who's Dan?' Deborah said.

'You know, Dan who lives here with us.'

'Sorry Rhys, I don't know who you're talking about,' she said.

Afterwards, he went to Vincent's room to ask the same question and got the same answer.

'Who's Dan?'

The fact that all the kids in the house were actors meant that they could stay pretty straight-faced and convincing, which made poor Rhys start to panic. That was the moment when my supposedly harmless prank took a wrong turn. Rhys dashed into his room to retrieve the print of the photo we'd taken together, but of course, I wasn't in it anymore. I'd vanished. It was like someone had tried to take a photograph of a ghost or a vampire that has no earthly image. Nothing. The picture was of Rhys and only Rhys. Now the poor kid was so shaken he burst into tears and then threw up. It was awful.

Suddenly everyone in the flat started rushing over to reassure him.

'No, no. It's alright! It was just a prank!'

Hearing all the fuss and realising something had gone wrong, I ran out of the bedroom. As soon as Rhys set eyes on me, he ran over and gave me a massive hug; he was so relieved. But, God, I felt so mean. What had I done?

Pretty soon after, Rhys laughed about it along with the rest of us. I still felt guilty about making him cry and throw up, but down the line we did all take the mickey out of him for totally falling for it.

In the end, there were so many pranks played during the show's run it was hard to know what was real and what wasn't. One day, Vincent had the metal door that led to the dressing room slammed on his hand, and started screaming about his finger being crushed. Vincent was like the boy who cried wolf, always pretending something terrible had happened, so instead of trying to help him or going over to see what was wrong, the rest of us just started laughing at him. The next thing we knew, he was in the toilet, crying, but knowing Vincent as I did, I still wasn't convinced he was on the level. That all changed when he came out of the toilet, holding up a finger that looked like it had been snapped in two. OK, so not a prank after all. Vincent had actually broken his finger. OOPS!

IT WAS HARD TO KNOW WHAT WAS REAL AND WHAT WASN'T

Meanwhile, I got pretty fit while doing that show, I'll tell you. It's not surprising. Apart from running around on stage every night, our dressing room was right at the top of the theatre. It was up about five flights of very narrow stairs, and we had to climb them several times a day. So it was a pretty decent workout!

At one point, there was a chance that I might have got kicked off the show altogether. It was a series of unfortunate events, one straight after the other, that meant I couldn't perform. First off, I was off one night due to illness; then I banged my leg on one of the mechanical props on the stage, then, a day or so later, I got a nasty migraine and couldn't do the second half of the show. It seems like every night, I had some sort of medical issue, but they were all completely genuine!

At the end of that week, I was back home, and that's when I got a call from the producers: 'Look, Dan, it feels to us like you might not want to be in the show. It seems a bit of a coincidence that three things have gone wrong within three days.'

Meanwhile, I was crying down the phone, 'No, I promise. I do want to do it! I'm fine, honest!'

When I went back the next week, everything was fine. I only missed one show for the rest of the whole year when I was just too ill to go on.

I loved the whole experience of doing that show, especially living right in the heart of London. I kind of think of it as my second home now, and I'd like to move back and spend some more time there as soon as I can. After we came out of lockdown in 2020, I went back for a long-overdue visit. When I wandered past the Theatre Royal, I had this overwhelming nostalgia and felt a bit teary-eyed.

I was in the show for a year, but because of the schedule, which sometimes changed at the last minute, it was hard for me to book any magic gigs. I couldn't commit to performing at someone's wedding or party when there was always the possibility that something would change and I'd have to let them down. I decided it was best not to do any at all and just concentrate on playing Mike Teavee. So, magic had to go on the back burner for a while, but I didn't abandon it completely.

I still enjoyed entertaining my mate Vincent and the other cast members with the odd trick.

For me, there was also a bit of magic within the show. My character has to disappear into thin air at one point in the story. In truth, I went down into a trapdoor on the stage. For that part of the show, the producers hired an illusionist, who also showed me how to make it all look real. I remember thinking, 'Wow! I'm doing magic live on stage every night in front of a huge West End audience.'

MAGIC HAD TO GO ON THE BACK BURNER FOR A WHILE

The illusionist and I got on very well, and we spent hours showing one another card tricks and getting all geeky about various illusions. There were even a few occasions when someone would have to intervene so I could get on with the job.

'Come on, Dan. Put the cards away. We're rehearsing now.'

We also had some very famous people come to watch the show, like Brian May from Queen, and the actor Colin Firth. After the show, they'd come backstage and say hello, and, of course, I'd make sure I got the chance to show them a quick card trick before they went.

Pretty soon, people were always asking me to show them tricks, from other cast members right through to members of the creative and production team. Finally, it got to the stage where if I wasn't acting or learning lines, I was doing tricks for someone. I remember once jokingly telling someone, 'I swear to God, when I leave this show, I'm going to send a massive invoice for all this extra entertainment.'

All in all, it was a fantastic experience and something I'd love to do more of. My mum ended up coming to watch the show about fifteen times – but then she's always been so supportive. Mum has always been very much of the mind that both my brother and I should think and dream big and follow our hearts and dreams. My dad's a bit different. His way of thinking is that if I can succeed in the things I love, then great, but that I shouldn't just rely on those things and pin all my hopes on them. He's a bit more realistic when it comes to stuff like that, and it's good to have both perspectives.

I learned a lot from my time in *Charlie*, and I realised how much of that skill I could put into my magic. When you're doing tricks for people, asking them to accept something their eyes can't believe, you have to be confident. You have to believe in what you're doing so that they can believe in it too. Performing magic tricks for people at shows and events isn't that different from acting.

Once I'd finished doing *Charlie And The Chocolate Factory*, I realised how much I'd missed being a magician. It was just something that was part of me, and I needed to get back to it.

Don't actually put the pen up your nose!

PEN UP THE NOSE

I used to do this trick in school, which would freak out my friends and teachers.

What you'll need: A pen or pencil. Your nose!

1 Put one end of a pen against one of your nostrils, pointing downward, and hold the other end between your fingers and thumb.

2 Slide your hand upwards over the pen until your fingertips reach your nose, giving the illusion that the pen is disappearing up your nostril. Make sure it looks like it's very painful!

3 Then, keeping the pen hidden, put your fingers to your lips and slide them down the pen to make it look like it's coming out of your mouth.

THE ART OF LEVITATION

I was chuffed when the guy from the Morrisons ad showed me how to do this. It's a great one for social media; perfect for an Instagram story!

What you'll need: Your own shoes! Someone else to film you.

1 Before you start filming, take one of your shoes off and place it line with the foot that still has a shoe on. Then angle your shoeless foot to the side of the shoe, so it can't be seen on camera.

2 Start filming as you slowly lift up onto tiptoe with the shoeless foot and raise your other foot (the one with the shoe) off the ground in full view of the camera – about an inch is enough. At the same time, grip and raise the empty shoe between the heel of your shoeless foot and your other foot.

Make sure you raise your arms at you go up, as if it's a magical gesture and in some way helping the levitation.

THE HOLE IN THE EAR

This one is sure to get a brilliant reaction from your friends and family.

What you'll need: Nothing apart from your ear, your thumb and index finger.

1 So no one can see what you're doing you need to cover your ear with your opposite hand during the set-up. Put your thumb against your ear, with the nail end facing forward. Grip the top of your ear with your forefinger and pull it downward.

2 Now hook your index finger under your earlobe and pull the two parts of your ear together.

3 Reveal your ear – it looks like your thumb has gone through it. Don't forget to wiggle your thumb and cry out as if you're in pain.

4 Then cover your ear again to pull your thumb out! Job done!

Give your ear a wiggle to make it look more convincing!

THE JACKET TRICK

Sometimes it's all in the outfit – if you're wearing a jacket and have trousers with a back pocket, then this is a great trick to have up your sleeve. See what I did there?

What you'll need: A jacket, a glass of water, a back pocket!

shhh!!

1 While no one is looking, carefully place a glass of water in your back pocket and cover it with your top.

2 Tell your audience you're going to make a glass of water appear from your jacket. You'll need to open your jacket first to show them there's nothing inside.

turn over

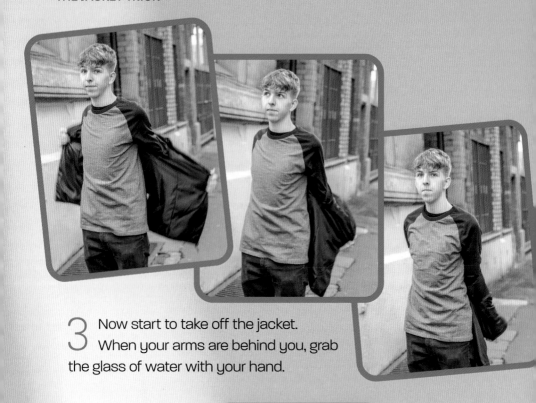

3 Now start to take off the jacket.
When your arms are behind you, grab
the glass of water with your hand.

4 Pull the glass carefully
through your sleeve as it turns inside
out, and then amaze everyone by pulling a
full glass of water out of your sleeve.

IF AT FIRST YOU DON'T SUCCEED

LAUGH UNTIL YOU DO

TRICKSTER

As I was getting older, I was starting to see that there were many occasions when magic could come in very handy. It often encouraged me to push the boundaries in certain areas, which worked in my favour. Some might call it taking liberties, but I'm sticking with pushing boundaries, OK?

I suppose it started during my journeys up and down to London for *Charlie and The Chocolate Factory*. I discovered a way to make the long, boring two-hour journey go with a bit more of a swing. I'd walk up and down the train, between carriages, doing card tricks for passengers. My gran was the one who often accompanied me on this trip, but she wasn't as keen on the idea.

I'D WALK UP AND DOWN THE TRAIN, DOING CARD TRICKS FOR PASSENGERS

'Don't be doing that all the time, you'll burn out!' she'd say. 'Don't forget, you've got a show to do tonight.'

As far as I was concerned, though, I was on to a good thing! Especially when I met Stan, a friendly bloke who worked on the trains and was regularly on duty when I travelled. He even allowed me into the first-class carriage to entertain the passengers, and nine times out of ten, I'd get a free upgrade to travel first class myself.

It was just one more reason why I never go anywhere without a pack of cards. They're always with me.

You'd be surprised how much free stuff you can get by doing a few tricks. I gave it a go with all sorts of stuff. Sweets, for instance, which I suppose is an obvious place to start when you're a kid. There was one particular sweet shop that I passed on my route to school every day – Sweets & Treats! I remember when it first opened; in I strolled with

I used magic to get out of maths!

a big cute grin on my face, with an offer I thought the owner couldn't possibly refuse.

'If I do a magic trick for you, do you think I might be able to get some sweets and freebies off you?'

The man behind the counter scratched his chin. 'Er . . . well . . .'

Look, if it's a rubbish trick, just be honest and tell me,' I said. 'I won't be offended and I don't expect something for nothing. Deal?'

The man nodded, clearly still not quite knowing what to make of this weird and confident young man standing at his counter.

'Alright, deal!' he said.

Needless to say, I walked out with a pocketful of free sweets!

After that, it kind of became a thing. Every day after school, I'd go into the shop and do tricks for free sweets. I was probably putting a bit of dent in his profits, but then again, this dude was probably making a heavy contribution to the decay of my teeth!

Ultimately, this also worked in chip shops, corner shops and in various other scenarios where I found myself short of change and in need of food. To me, this was the best thing ever, but it set me thinking about what other benefits might be gained from magic. By now I was at secondary school, so that seemed a good place to start.

OK, so some of my dodges at school weren't exactly magic. Like the times I cut holes in my maths textbook, just big enough for my phone to fit in. If I was careful enough, anyone who looked over at me would think I was studying the book. Meanwhile, I was sneakily using the calculator on my phone to solve a problem.

One time, a supply teacher in a maths class, who was quite strict, caught me eating chocolate buttons.

'Are you eating in my class?' she called out.

'No,' I said, all innocent.

'Well, what's that in your hand?'

'Nothing.'

'I can see you've got something,' she said. 'Show me what it is.'

With a bit of magic, I made the chocolate disappear in front of her eyes. When I did, she went from annoyed to amazed.

'What? How did you do that?'

Being a supply teacher, she had no idea I was a magician. But once she knew, she just wanted to see more tricks. So, after that, I pulled out a pack of cards and spent the entire forty minutes of the lesson doing card tricks for the

I PULLED OUT A PACK OF CARDS AND SPENT THE ENTIRE LESSON DOING CARD TRICKS

teacher and the class. She was so engrossed she completely lost track of time. When the bell went for the end of the lesson, she looked a bit panicky.

'Don't tell anyone else I let you do magic tricks for an entire lesson,' she said. 'I'll be in big trouble.'

I was a hero for the rest of that week as far as the rest of my class was concerned. They were over the moon that I'd distracted the teacher and freed them from an afternoon of boring maths problems.

Another time, I'd been given a detention for not handing in my homework. So, in an attempt to get out of it, I made a bargain with an unsuspecting teacher, who agreed that if I could identify a card they'd named, they would guarantee my freedom. I tried that one a few times, although some of the teachers weren't having any of it.

Don't get me wrong; it wasn't that I didn't like school. It's just that I was sort of on another planet most of the time. I was always thinking

about new tricks or staring at a pack of cards under my desk, just out of the eye-line of the teachers, showing the kids around me what tricks I could do. In the end, I had to stop taking my cards to school because they became too much of a distraction.

I remember one of my teachers told me that I had zero chance of making it as a professional magician and that the only way I was going to get by in life was to do a 'normal' job, whatever that might be! I used that as motivation to prove the teacher wrong. If ever I felt like I wasn't putting in the hours or practising hard enough, I'd remind myself what that teacher had said and use it to get my butt in gear!

Around that time, I noticed that young and up-and-coming performers of all sorts were posting more and more content online – and there were quite a few magicians among them. Right, I thought, let's have a go at this. I already had quite a few videos on my YouTube channel, but now I started taking it a bit more seriously.

One of the things I noticed was that, in the past, magicians tended to post videos where they were performing tricks to another person or a group of people in the street or at a party. That was fine, but the ones I liked watching were of solo magicians performing straight to the camera. This meant that the viewer wasn't just watching someone else enjoying the trick; it was as if it was being done only to them. The magician was talking directly to the viewer. So, that's how I started to make my videos – close up and personal – breaking the fourth wall and asking my audience questions as if I was there in the room with them. That's not to say I always made my videos on my own – I was soon roping in lots of friends to be in them too – but even when there was one other person in the video with me, I tried to make sure that much of the action was directed at the camera and at the audience.

Once I'd decided on my style, I posted a lot of videos, and I mean a *lot*! And I was happy to see many of them getting lots of views, likes and positive comments.

Eventually, my YouTube channel grabbed the attention of some production scouts who were on the lookout for young people to appear on an American TV show. That's right! Completely out of the blue, we got a message with an offer for my mum and I to fly to LA for a TV show called *Little Big Shots*, created and hosted by the actor and comedian Steve Harvey. This was a huge deal. Not only was it in America, but the first season of the show had been the NBC network's most-watched show in ten years, with more than thirteen million viewers. Plus, Steve Harvey is a bit of a legend as far as American TV goes. At the time he was hosting one of their biggest TV game shows, *Family Feud*, and he's appeared in all sorts of other TV shows and movies as well as having been a stand-up comedian for nearly thirty years. No pressure then!

I was thirteen and this felt like a massive thing at the time. The idea of flying to LA, to actual Hollywood, was really exciting. The wide streets, the palm trees, the Hollywood Walk of Fame . . . Actually, I'm not sure who was the most excited, me or my mum!

The deal was that would get an all-expenses nine-day trip to LA, just to do this one show. We were staying at the Hilton Hotel, and the fact that we had so much time off meant that we were able to do plenty of exploring and visit some of the great tourist stuff the city has to offer.

Universal Studios, of course, was a favourite, and while I was at the Wizarding World of Harry Potter there, I felt right at home.

'I'm a wizard myself, so this feels right,' I told my mum. 'It feels good to be here.'

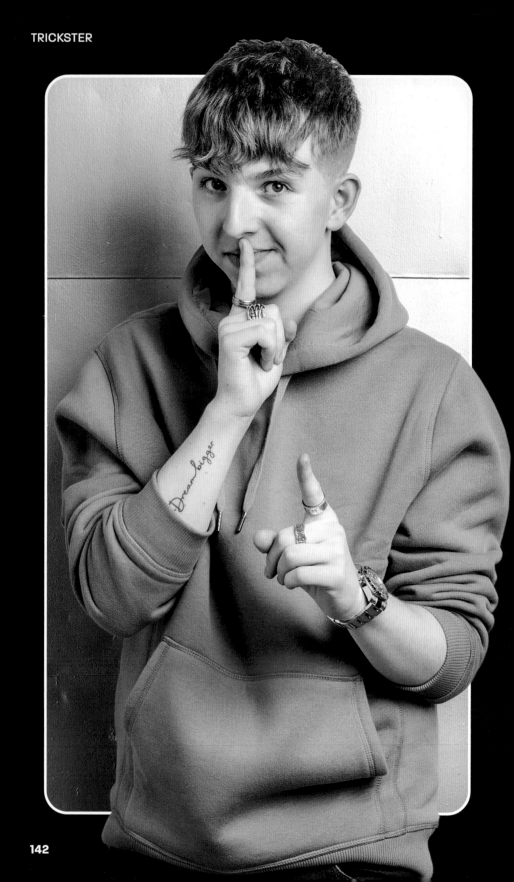

While we in the wand shop a guide picked me out of the crowd during his grand introduction to the store.

'Have you got a wand, sir?'

'No, I don't have one,' I said.

'Ah, then come to the front with me, and we'll see what we can do about that,' he said.

'Yeah, but I'm a real wizard, so I don't need one,' I said, and then I showed him a card trick.

'Well, you're definitely not a muggle,' he said. 'I still think you're worthy of a wand.'

Before the actual recording of *Little Big Shots*, there were a couple of days of rehearsals where I met kids from different parts of the world who were also going to appear on the show. There were American kids, of course, but also kids from Ukraine, Mexico and various other countries. It was quite a cool thing meeting and mixing with them all, thousands of miles away from our own homes.

The show itself couldn't have gone better. After my performance, Steve Harvey said I was 'the greatest magician', and the lovely audience gave me a standing ovation. I'd arrived!

One cool thing that happened while we were there was getting a VIP pass to The Magic Castle, which is a performance space and private club in Hollywood. It's especially for magicians and people who are really into magic. In fact, it's supposed to be *the* place to go if you're a magician in LA .

To become a fully-fledged member of The Magic Castle, you have to be a practising magician with magic either as a career or serious hobby. Even then, you must audition in front of the membership committee, who decide whether or not you can be let into the inner sanctum! The only reason we managed to get a pass was because one of the women who worked in the wardrobe department on *Little Big Shots* knew someone who was a member and who could get us the special invitation.

We were told that on most evenings at the castle, they have a few different magic acts performing, but as well as that, you can also have dinner in the restaurant or drinks in one of the bars. All sorts of magicians and variety acts perform there in one of several different spaces, some large and some small. There's even a gallery for close-up magic – the kind of stuff I do.

The thing is, you're only allowed in if you're a member or the guest of a member, so it's not one of those places that everybody knows about – especially as the entrance of the place has no visible doors leading to the inside. Mum said it reminded of her of the house from *The Addams Family*. In fact, it's so secret that visitors have to say a

A BOOKSHELF OPENS, REVEALING A PASSAGE INTO THE HOUSE

special phrase to a statue of an owl with flashing eyes in order to be granted entry. Once you've done that, a bookshelf opens, revealing a passage into the house.

The place bills itself as 'the most unusual private club in the world', and I could definitely see why. It had this real old-fashioned nightclub vibe – the sort of thing you might see in an old black-and-white film. The décor was all quite dark and gothic, just like you'd imagine a castle to be, and the walls were covered in newspaper cuttings, old posters, and pictures of some of the performers who had been part of the club's history. There was even a dress code, which was strictly

formal or party attire. Apparently, you couldn't just turn up in jeans and trainers. That would definitely be a no-no, even if you did know the secret phrase to say to the owl with the flashing eyes.

Anyway, we were told before we went that the men all wore suits and ties and the women wore dresses – and this rule had to be adhered to. Well, I hadn't taken a suit with me to LA, so we had to travel to a mall, thirty minutes away from where were staying, so that I could buy one.

When we eventually got there, I was slightly put out to find that there were actually very few people in formal gear, so we'd gone and bought a brand-new suit for nothing!

By this time, I was starting to make a name for myself in magic circles and it wasn't long after the LA trip that a friend told me that

CAN YOU IMAGINE SEEING YOUR ABSOLUTE HERO TALKING ABOUT YOU LIKE THAT IN AN INTERVIEW

he'd watched an interview with Dynamo and he'd actually mentioned me! Really? Surely, my friend was joking! Of course, I had to see the clip – and when I did, I was amazed to find it was true. I couldn't believe it when I heard him mentioning my name and saying he thought I had a lot of character and charisma and would go far.

Can you imagine seeing your absolute hero talking about you like that in an interview? To say I was buzzing would be an understatement. I think that's when I thought; I can do this. If someone like Dynamo believes that about me, I can make it as a professional magician.

DAN'S
FIVE RULES FOR LIFE!

1 Have fun! Nothing is worth doing unless you're having fun.

4 Try your best not to compare yourself to other people. Easier said than done, believe me I know! But everyone is on their own journey, so focus on you. After all, you're the main character in the movie of your life!

2 Try and live in the moment. I struggle with that sometimes, when I'm trying to achieve a distant goal, but the journey there is just as exciting and important as the end result.

5 Remember, family is the most important thing. Well . . . after magic tricks. (I'm joking of course.) Tell your family you love them and cherish the moments you have.

3 Be kind! It sounds like a cliché, but you should always do your best to treat people as you want to be treated. What I'm trying to say is, do nice things for others and it will come back to you!

A few months later, I was performing at an event where I met a presenter from Heart Radio. After telling her what a massive fan of Dynamo I was, she told me she was interviewing him on her show the following week and asked if I'd like to come down to the station. What me? Talk to Dynamo on the radio? As you can probably imagine, I jumped at the chance of interviewing my hero. On the day, I wasn't even that nervous, and we ended up having a proper good chat.

About a week later, I finally met him in person at his book signing. He recognised me as soon as he saw me, then stood up and hugged me.

'Dan, how are you?'

It was such a weird feeling getting to see my idol up close. It was the first time I'd experienced something like that. I remember thinking at the time how I'd love to be famous and successful enough to do a book, just like Dynamo had. It's funny thinking back to that now because here I am writing my own book. I guess it just goes to prove that if you have a dream of doing something, you should keep dreaming and keep going for it. Who knows? Maybe I'll be sitting down and reading your book one day in the future.

After doing the American version of *Little Big Shots*, I was invited to appear on the British version, hosted by the brilliantly funny Dawn French. I don't think I was all that nervous; I certainly don't seem to be, looking back at the video clip. I started off by tapping her on the forehead and telling her to name the first card that came to her – she picked two of hearts. Now, before the show I'd drawn a series of stick-man magicians in black marker on the back of each card in the pack so they would make a little cartoon movie when you flicked through them. Then I found the two of hearts in amongst the pack and held it up for her.

PAUL DANIELS

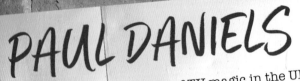

Paul Daniels is a legend of TV magic in the UK. I guess you'd say he was pretty old school as far as magicians go – his style was very much in the vein of classic conjuring – but still so impressive and a brilliant entertainer. He paved the way for so many other TV magicians and I remember seeing a lot of him when I was a young kid.

Reading up on Paul, I realised there were quite a few things about him that I could identify with. He's from near Middlesbrough, so another northern boy, and, as a child he was quite shy and awkward. Before magic, he'd found it difficult to communicate with people but, suddenly, he was able to connect in a way he'd never thought possible. That's something I can definitely understand.

He also started young – he did his first magic show when he was fourteen – although his first TV appearance wasn't until nearly twenty years later on *Opportunity Knocks*, which was basically like the *X Factor* of its time. By the 1980s he had his own primetime show, which ran for fifteen years.

Paul did some amazing magic on the show – even recreating some of the stunts of the brilliant showman Harry Houdini. Houdini performed throughout the UK in the early twentieth century and his outstanding feats of daring and escapology have become legendary all over the world.

The stand-out trick from Paul for me was his cup-and-ball sequence. The way it was structured was so masterful, and I remember thinking that he must have spent so many hours perfecting it.

'Now I didn't influence your choice, did I?' I said. 'I know it wouldn't take a lot to influence you.'

'You're so right!' she said, laughing. 'It would basically take a gin and tonic!'

After that, I flicked through the pack, revealing the very last stickman drawing on the very last card. I held it up: two of hearts.

'You're pretty good, aren't you?' she said.

'I'm alright,' I replied casually, then launched into another trick.

I have to say, Dawn was really lovely, making me feel relaxed and giving me the space to be a bit cheeky and funny with her. Getting my personality across and building a rapport with my audience is crucial for me, whether it's a gig, a small private event or a national TV show. I always feel like my experiences when I was acting have helped with that side of things. For me, the personality comes first and the magic second. You don't want to watch someone who's just saying, 'Ha! I've just done something that you don't understand!' No one can relate to that, and it would probably be quite boring to watch someone perform tricks with no flair or character to make their act unique. In fact, I would say to anyone wanting to perform magic that one of the most important things is having fun with it and making it your own. Don't make it purely about the trick or the reveal; make it about the performance surrounding it, and think about really entertaining your audience – keeping them enthralled and with you all the way along.

After I'd been on both *Little Big Shots*, I remember thinking, 'That's it! I've made it now. I've been on two TV shows, one in America and one in the UK.' Maybe I'd even end up becoming a modern-day Paul Daniels, who, back in the day, had been the most famous magician on British TV. Ah, if only it were that easy!

PULSE STOP

This seems like quite a scary trick, although no harm is done while you're performing it.

What you'll need: A squashy ball – something like a stress ball.

1 Before the trick, pop the ball under your arm, concealed under your top or T-shirt!

stick it up your jumper!

2 Using the wrist of the same arm, ask your participant to find your pulse and count the beats out loud as they feel them: 1, 2, 3, 4, 5 . . .

3 When they get to five, sneakily squeeze the ball in your armpit as hard as you can. After a few seconds they will stop counting, unable to feel the pulse. After another few seconds, release the pressure on the ball and the pulse will start again. Oh yes, you can actually stop your own heartbeat – or at least give an illusion of that!

BLISTERED!

Another one that's perfect for social media, or to prank your friends and family. This one is all about acting!

What you'll need: The cap of a marker pen, a frying pan. Erm . . . and I guess being near a cooker would help too!

shhh!

1 A minute or so before doing the trick, push the cap of the marker pen really hard onto the top of your finger and hold for a while. When you take it off, it should leave a white mark that looks like a blister on your finger.

Owww!!

2 Hold up the pan and without anyone seeing the 'blister', place your finger on the pan and shout out as if the pan is hot and you're in pain because you've burnt yourself. A little dramatic, I know.

3 Show the blister to your sympathetic audience. Remember to really lay it on thick about how much it hurts.

4 Sneakily rub your thumb on the blister, it will disappear in four or five seconds, then shock them again when you reveal your magically un-blistered finger!

PHONE IN A BALLOON

This is such a flexible trick because it works with all sorts of everyday objects so you can do it at any time with whatever is around.

What you'll need: A phone (or something a similar shape and size). An un-inflated balloon.

1 Take a balloon and blow it up, then hold the nozzle so the air doesn't escape.

2 With your free hand, pick up the phone. So, now you are holding the inflated balloon in one hand by the nozzle, and the phone in the other, flat in your palm. Lift the balloon above the phone.

3 Gradually bring the balloon down, pressing it onto the phone and letting the air out. As the ballon deflates, the rubber will wrap around the phone.

turn over →

Pull the nozzle
and snap it back
to help with the
illusion that the
phone is inside

4 The balloon will wrap around the phone as it deflates, creating the illusion that the phone has actually gone inside it.

5 Now hold the phone up, making sure you don't expose the side where part of the phone will be visible through a gap in the balloon.

6 Finally, blow into the nozzle to inflate the balloon again, creating the illusion that the phone has penetrated the baloon. This one looks like real magic!

THE JAFFA CAKE TRICK

This is a great one for social media – I called my video the insane cake trick!

What you'll need: a pack of Jaffa Cakes work well and two identical coins.

1 Beforehand you need to take a coin and stick it all the way inside a Jaffa Cake then put the Jaffa cake back in its box.

shhh!!

2 Pick up the other coin and pretend to place it in your opposite hand, but actually just drop it. Then give that hand a magic blow before opening it, to reveal it's empty.

3 Take the Jaffa Cake back out of the box and break it to reveal the coin inside.

COIN IN A PEN CAP

This one will take a little practice but is worth it!

What you'll need: A pen with a cap, a coin.

1 Place the coin in the palm of your left hand (if you're right handed) and tap it with the pen.

shhh!!

2 Tap it again and then on the next tap, during the motion of tapping the coin and bringing your right-hand back up, throw the coin into the palm of your right hand, where you can hold it with the pen. It looks like the coin has disappeared.

3 Remove the cap of the pen without dropping or showing the coin, and shake the cap above your left hand.

4 Now let the coin drop from your hand, creating the illusion that the coin has come out of the cap of the pen. Finish the trick by showing them that the coin could not possibly have fitted in the cap of the pen without magic!

SOME THINGS ARE BETTER LEFT A

MYSTERY

TEENAGE YEARS

Being at school meant I needed to find just the right balance between practising magic tricks and keeping on top of all my school work. 'How did you do that?' I hear you ask! Well, the truth is, I didn't really. School and studies always came second to magic, so I got into a fair bit of trouble for not delivering my homework on time. The fact was, I loved magic and hated school. It was as simple as that.

I needed to get better at magic, though, and to keep mastering new tricks and illusions. Right through secondary school, I was getting gigs at parties and events. As far as I was concerned, I was already working, and I was happy with that. As time went on, however, I started to feel like there could be so much more.

I knew my TV appearances had come about because I'd put my magic out there online, so that was definitely the way to get noticed. What I needed to figure out now was, how could I make my online presence grow? How could I reach an even bigger audience? TV shows certainly didn't come around every day, so social media was the way forward. I was sure of that.

HOW COULD I REACH AN EVEN BIGGER AUDIENCE?

I'd often see other YouTubers and content makers with hundreds of thousands of views and even more subscribers, but after a year of posting video on Instagram, I only had around 10,000 followers plus 100 subscribers on YouTube. OK, so 10,000 Instagram followers was a decent amount, but there had to be a way to make this whole thing bigger.

A lot of my ideas for content would come from just walking around and observing what's going on around me. Like, if I was in a supermarket or shop, I might see something that sparked an idea for a

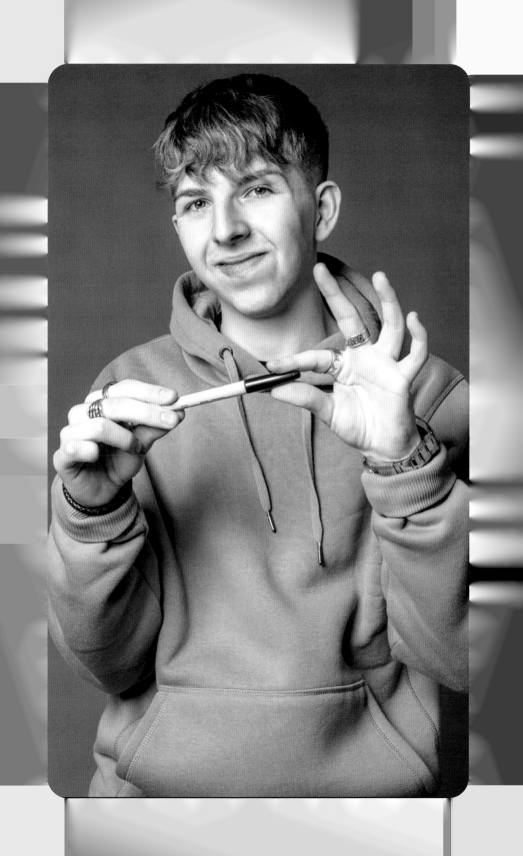

trick or a video and then somehow incorporate it. There are some key elements I stuck to – which I'll talk about later in the book – but I didn't really have a set formula when it came to making creative choices. Back then, I sometimes I used to tell myself that I wasn't a creative person. The trouble is, when you reinforce those negative ideas about yourself, they can stick in your head. So, if you tell yourself you're not creative, you're not leaving the doors open for any kind of creativity to come in. These days, I suppose I think of creativity as being like a muscle. And, like all muscles, it needs exercise!

Eventually, I started to think differently; to think positively about how inventive I could be. I knew I wasn't trying to re-invent the wheel per se, I just wanted to present things in a slightly different way to anything I'd seen before – in my own style.

I JUST WANTED TO PRESENT THINGS IN A SLIGHTLY DIFFERENT WAY

Mostly, I tried to let it come naturally. I think that's when my videos and posts really started to work.

One of the things I did was to get some help and advice from other magicians I admired online; people who were doing something similar to me, but with much more success. I've heard people say that social media can be a blessing or a curse, but, from my experience, it's generally been a good thing. I've met some of my best friends on various social media platforms – some of them fellow magicians.

One of them was Luca Gallone, a young British magician who, at the time, had 60,000 followers on Instagram. That seemed to me like a huge number! I contacted Luca, thinking he was like some magician superhero, and asked if he would be up for a chat with me, perhaps

CRISS ANGEL

Criss Angel is another magician whose videos I've loved watching – so amazing! What is different about Criss is that he takes these big, stage illusions – like sawing someone in half – and does them on the street. His style of magic has always been brilliantly flashy and impressive, and as well as being an illusionist, he's also a very talented musician.

Criss, from New York, once spent 24 hours chained up underwater in a water-torture cell the size of a phone box in Times Square. Another time, he escaped from a hotel before its demolition in front of a crowd of about 50,000 people. He's had his own TV show – *Criss Angel Mindfreak* – where he walked on water, cut himself in half in full view of an audience, walked up the side of a hotel in Las Vegas and got run over by a steamroller while lying on a bed of broken glass. It's no real surprise that he was crowned magician of the decade in 2009.

Of course, when you're performing tricks as wild and crazy as this, there's always the potential for things to go badly wrong. In his 2017 Las Vegas show, he attempted an aerial trick where he hung upside down in a straitjacket. One night, he lost consciousness mid-air in front of a fully packed auditorium and had to be helped down and rushed to hospital. Amazingly he was back on stage doing the same stunt a day later!

I'm also down with Criss's philosophy on life, as it's quite similar to my own. He tells his fans that, 'Anything is possible' if they believe – in themselves, in magic, in life. That's pretty cool, right?

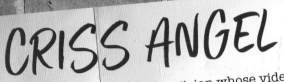

giving me a few tips on becoming as successful as he was. Luca was a great help to me in building my social-media presence. We ended up becoming good friends, even filming some videos together.

It works both ways too. At the end of 2018, I made another friend online, a young Australian guy called Ash Hodgkinson. When I watched his Insta videos, he reminded me of myself. He was just a year older than me and putting out great videos, but still relatively new to social media, trying to build his fanbase. This time, it was my turn to help someone, passing on what I'd already learned, sharing some of my tips over FaceTime. Eventually, we spoke every day, but with the time difference, my evenings were his early morning and vice versa. It sometimes felt weird, becoming such close friends with someone I'd never met, but after a year, Ash flew from the other side of the world and stayed with my family for two weeks.

My point here is: don't ever be scared to reach out and send someone a message! You might be a couple of short messages away from making a new friend – maybe even a friend for life!

At the beginning of 2019, when I was fifteen, I finally got my shot at doing *Britain's Got Talent*, It was one of the most nerve-wracking things I've ever done. Before I stepped on stage in front of that huge live audience – not to mention the millions of people that would be watching me on TV – my heart was pumping, I was sweating, I felt like my legs were all wobbly beneath me. I was an absolute wreck! A few seconds after stepping on stage, though, the nerves had evaporated. I loved it!

To be honest, sawing people in half wasn't exactly in my repertoire, but I was willing to give it a go. After all magicians had been sawing women in half on stage for nearly a hundred years, if not since ancient Egyptian times as is sometimes believed. Officially, though, the world first witnessed a woman being sawn in half in 1921, when P. T. Selbit cut through a box containing his female assistant at a north London theatre.

IT LOOKED LIKE SOME DODGY CARDBOARD PACKING BOX WITH A SAW ATTACHED TO IT

I wanted the box I used to look homemade. I worked on my own design, sticking bits of cardboard and paper on it and writing my own handmade 'Dan Rhodes Magic' sign with a marker pen. By the time Ant and Dec wheeled it on for me in front of a slightly horrified judging panel, it looked like some dodgy cardboard packing box with a saw attached to it. I didn't see the point of going with an illusion that looked so professional that it was bound to work. For me, the beauty of it was going on with this tatty homemade thing, so there would be some jeopardy as to whether it might go horribly wrong.

'I never had the budget to do an amazing illusion, so I've actually made this one myself,' I said to the panel.

'I can see that,' Amanda said.

They were all laughing, but I definitely detected an air of panic among them too.

When I invited Amanda on stage to help me perform the illusion, she looked rather nervous, especially as she was climbing into the box.

Just before sawing the lovely Amanda in half, Simon pressed his buzzer, and up went the big red X – meaning he wasn't a fan. I'd seen that buzzer used on the show over the years, but I never guessed how loud it was – it gave me the fright of my life. In that moment I realised I had two choices: option one was to break down or walk off the stage, option two was to laugh it off and keep on going. Looking back, I'm so glad I went with option two.

Still, the trick went off like a dream, and once it was done, as far as everyone could see, I had indeed sawed *Britain's Got Talent* judge Amanda Holden clean in half. But, of course, before I put her back together, I needed to be sure of one thing.

'Now, depending on your answer, I may or may not put you back together,' I warned her. 'Is it a yes, or is it a no?'

'It's a yes from me,' she said.

At that point, I dropped down on one knee as if I were proposing.

'Thank you!' I said, 'I thought I might be a bit young for you, but thank you very much anyway.'

After the illusion was done, Simon retracted the buzz and laughed.

'Sorry Dan, I thought by buzzing things would go wrong, but that didn't work.'

Amanda gave him a playful slap.

I walked away with four yeses from the judges that day, and Simon telling me I had 'showmanship'. Job done!

I love *Britain's Got Talent* as a show, and do I really appreciate the opportunity doing it gave me. Plus, it got me my social media 'verified' blue tick, which was my biggest goal as a kid – LOL! Still at the end of the day, it's a TV show first and talent show second. I think you have to be aware of that with any TV talent show. It's inevitable that the things that makes the best TV, good or bad, will often win out and get the most coverage. That's just the nature of the business.

Ultimately, my appearance on primetime TV didn't have as much impact on my social media stats as I hoped it might. That was something I was just going to have to continue building on my own! But how?

Magicians have been wowing theatre audiences with live magic shows since the Victorian era, when magic went mainstream. Well, now it was my turn! Not long before my sixteenth birthday, I performed my first real magic show. It was in the function room of a restaurant called Bella Vista, which wasn't too far from my home. This wasn't like the other gigs I'd done, where I'd turn up at a wedding or a party and then go around performing close-up magic for the guests. This was an actual show. On a stage. A show that a hundred people had paid to come and see. And it was sold out!

OK, so I'll admit that the main reason it sold out was because of all my mum's Facebook friends – family, mates, old work colleagues – who'd all bought tickets. So, it wasn't me who'd sold out the show; it was my mum!

Joel
ON DAN

When I first met Dan, I was instantly aware that he was different to the other magicians I had met. His drive, curiosity, and persistence are just some of the things that make him so special.

It's easy to look at someone like Dan and think, 'He just got lucky.' I can tell you wholeheartedly, from watching Dan closely over five years, that he's the most diligent, obsessed, hard-working person I know. There's no magic trick behind his success. And knowing Dan, he's just getting started.

Shame about his annoying Manchester accent. ;)

Love you lots mate!

It was around then that I first spoke to fellow magician and YouTuber Joel M, who I also discovered on social media. He was one of the few magicians at the time, like myself, posting magic content on Instagram. His videos, in my opinion, were the best. As well as making videos, I could also see that Joel regularly performed his magic on stage. So, I shot him a DM that went something along the lines of, 'Hi Joel, love your videos, my friend, and would absolutely love to jump on a call sometime.'

To my surprise, he graciously accepted, and we spoke the very next day. During the call, we chatted about life, magic and many other things. I told him I had a live show coming up and asked if he'd be up for sharing any advice. We've been mates ever since, and we FaceTime every couple of days. In fact, I would say Joel is my best friend. However, I still haven't been able to master an impersonation of his heavy Irish accent!

Even after speaking with Joel, I was still pretty nervous before the show; performing on stage for an

> ## WHEN THE TIME CAME, I JUST THREW MYSELF INTO IT, GIVING IT EVERYTHING I HAD

hour with a hundred-strong seated audience was a whole new ball game. Scary as hell! Beforehand, the adrenaline was pumping; my legs went numb. But when the time came, I just threw myself into it, giving it everything I had. Which, looking back, might have been a bit too much!

I remember at one point early on in the show, seeing my brother Harrison signalling for me to slow down, but I couldn't really grasp what he was going on about, so I just kept going. I'd meticulously

rehearsed an hour's worth of magic tricks for this show, allowing time for audience participation, getting people up on stage, and all that jazz. After thirty-five minutes, though, I realised to my horror that I'd almost come to the end of my set. My adrenaline was so full-on, it had propelled me through at warp speed, and I'd just about finished my entire show with twenty-five minutes still to go. I couldn't think how it had happened or what everyone must be thinking. It was like I'd drunk ten strong coffees. I mean, I talk pretty fast anyway, but I must have literally been going at double speed.

I looked out into the audience for signs of confusion on people's faces, but no ... everyone looked like they were still with me – and enjoying it. So, keen to make sure I gave people their money's worth, I just started improvising. I literally came up with tricks on the spot for the last half of the show. I suppose, having done a lot of close-up magic at parties, it wasn't too difficult. The audience were none the wiser either, thinking this was just a different section of the show – the second half – with no clue I was just making it all up as I went along. The funny thing is, some of the improvised tricks I did, wandering among the crowd, got the best reaction of all that night. Ultimately, everyone had a great time. They loved it.

> MY ADRENALINE WAS SO FULL-ON, IT HAD PROPELLED ME THROUGH AT WARP SPEED

It was an excellent lesson to pace myself in future. Set myself times for tricks and not let the adrenaline take over during a live show. Not that there were going to many of those over the next couple of years. Not with a global pandemic on the horizon!

THE VICTORIANS

The Victorian era was the age of the great illusionists. This was a time when magic moved into the world of variety shows and theatre, and also into the fairground, where it became a massive part of Victorian entertainment.

This was the beginning of modern conjuring, and it is a French man who was known professionally Robert-Houdin, who is considered the father of this style of magic. In fact, his illusions in the mid-Victorian era were so clever and amazing, he was forced to reveal all his secrets to the police, just so he didn't get prosecuted for witchcraft!

Two magicians called John Maskelyne and George Cooke became famous in the late nineteenth century, after Maskelyne had seen American spiritualists the Davenport Brothers perform and worked out how their 'spirit cabinet' worked. He worked with his friend Cooke to make a replica cabinet and together they created a show that revealed the Davenports' performance as a trick as well as developing some other illusions of their own. By the 1870s, Maskelyne and Cook were the biggest magic act in the UK. They performed hugely popular magic shows along with the ventriloquists, quick-change artists, and also the up-and-coming magicians they'd chosen to take under their wing and support. They didn't always get it right, though! They famously refused Harry Houdini a place on their bill in 1898, just two years before his own show in London, when he took the world of magic and illusion by storm. Big mistake!

When people think of a magician, they often think of a man. Until the mid-nineteenth century women magicians were practically unheard of. However, as magic performances became more and more a part of Victorian entertainment, women started working as magicians too, sometimes performing by them-selves but more often alongside their husbands or other members of their family. These days the world of magic is open to everyone, just shoot a video and off you go!

THE REBORN CAN ILLUSION

This is one of my personal favourites, because it's one you can do up close in person, or on social media.

What you'll need: An un-opened can of soft drink, a whiteboard pen with black ink.

1 Before you perform the trick, prepare the can by using the pen to black out the area of the top that you drink from, so it looks like the can has been opened.

colour in here!!

2 Show your participant the 'open' can and then tilt it downward to show that no liquid is coming out – now you've really convinced them that the can's empty.

3 With your thumb, sneakily rub off the black ink, then snap your fingers to reveal the magically 'reborn' can.

turn over

4 Open the can, pour out the drink, and wait for the reaction.

THE VANISHING TOOTHPICK

I like this trick because it uses ordinary things you can find around the house.

What you'll need: A toothpick, sticky tape, scissors.

1 To prepare for the trick, cut off off a small square of tape, and stick the toothpick to your thumbnail so it points downward toward your wrist.

2 It's simple! When you curl your thumb forward, the toothpick is there . . .

3 . . . but when you open your hand, it disappears behind your thumb. Magic!

APPEARING GLASSES

This is probably one of my coolest tricks because it involves wearing sunglasses. It's another good one for social media!

What you'll need: Any pair of glasses – they don't have to be sunglasses!

1 Hide the glasses behind your flat hands, hooking your thumbs over the top of them and making sure the arms of the glasses are extended, but hidden behind your hands.

shhh!!

2 Move your hands (and the hidden glasses) slowly up to your face until they are covering your eyes.

3 Pop your hands away in a flash, revealing glasses over your eyes

BOOM!!!

Add a sound effect for dramatic impact.

MAGIC WATER

A good trick for a social-media post and very easy! Just don't let anyone drink the water afterwards! I will NOT be held responsible! LOL!

What you'll need: A bottle of water and some good-quality art paint – any colour you like, I sometimes use orange to say I'm turning the water into orange juice.

1 To prepare the trick beforehand, take the cap off the bottle and place a little paint inside the cap. Screw the cap back on.

2 Show your
audience the
bottle of clear water.

3 As soon as you shake it, the paint will hit the water and 'magically' colour it.

MUNDUS VULT DECIPI, ERGO

DECIPIATUR

(The world wants to be deceived, so let it be deceived)

SOCIAL MEDIA STAR

When TikTok came along, it definitely grabbed my attention. It was new, different, and people my age seemed to respond to it. I got quite excited about the idea of a brand-new platform. Still, nothing much happened when I opened an account and uploaded some of my videos from Instagram. No traffic. Maybe this wasn't the right one for me after all?

By then, I'd left school and was going to college. I'd started off doing a media course, which turned out to be something very different to what I'd imagined. It just wasn't the right fit for me. I felt like I was biding my time. I'd just turned sixteen and I had to be in full time education until I was eighteen, but my heart wasn't really in what I was doing. What I really wanted to do was to be a magician!

A week or so after coming to the sad conclusion that TikTok might not be for me, I woke up one morning to find that my video that showed me making a bottle disappear had reached over 200,000 views. What?!! Up till that point, I'd never had anywhere near that many views on anything. What was going on?

IN THE END, THAT VIDEO GOT A MILLION VIEWS, WHICH WAS INSANE.

In a week, I had 10,000 TikTok followers, which had taken me a whole year on Instagram. I was definitely onto something. In the end, that video got a million views, which was insane.

Not longer after, the Covid pandemic hit and we went into lockdown. It's no surprise that the demand for online content went through the roof. A massive amount of the world's population was off school or work, shut away in their homes for months on end. After a few weeks, we'd binged watched our box sets and all our Netflix

shows, and everyone was desperately looking for something new. So much of the entertainment world went online, with people doing their thing from their living rooms and bedrooms because there was nowhere else to do it.

It's funny, even though TikTok was becoming much more popular, there hadn't been too much magic happening on it up to that point. Maybe that was why my bottle video had taken off. I mean, I'd been trying for over a year to get a million views on an Instagram video, but now, with TikTok, things were happening a lot faster.

At first, I'd been doing a video every couple of weeks, then one a week, but, during the pandemic, I upped it to one a day! I mean, what else did I have to do apart from creating videos? And because the restrictions meant I wasn't able to get close enough to anyone else to have them in my videos, I *had* to get creative! That was when I started trying out all sorts of different things. I did my usual card and coin tricks to the camera, but I also did some fortune-telling vids, where I'd throw a ball into a cup and ask it questions. Then there were the mathematical mind-reading videos, and the behind-the-scenes videos where I taught tricks and gave away secrets. I threw everything I had it. Some ideas worked really well, and some fell a little bit flat, but it was a real learning curve for me to see what was working and what wasn't – and vitally important. I guess there was a consistency in what I was doing that people latched on to. The videos were fast, funny, and left people wanting more. The more content I posted, the more I learned about what people were reacting to the most.

My TikTok followers grew and grew. I went from 200,000 to a million in less than a year; the day I hit that million mark was one the best days of my life.

It was a perfect storm, really. With TikTok blowing up and everyone on their phones during various lockdowns, I poured all my time into making magic and posting videos. In the end, I was basically in my room making videos nine-to-five most days; it had suddenly become my day job, even though I wasn't making any money from it. With college closed, I had nowhere to go and we were given little to no college work to study at home either. I really had nothing else to do except to try to entertain all the other people who were stuck at home, just like me.

By the time I was back at college, having changed to drama from media, I was so into my routine of video-making that I couldn't seem to find the time to do the reading or learn scripts for my course. This meant that I'd sometimes end up with teachers having a go at me for not being on top of things. The thing was, I was getting a reaction from what I was doing at home. I was building something and I could see it blooming and growing in front of my eyes, day by day. The college drama course was just that, a course. I didn't feel like it was going to lead me anywhere; it was just something I had to do. It wasn't that I was being lazy or rebellious, I just wanted to concentrate on what I knew was going to be my career.

I WAS BUILDING SOMETHING AND I COULD SEE IT BLOOMING AND GROWING

Still, putting out that much content wasn't always easy, and it took discipline. In fact, it usually sucked up a big chunk of my day – and still does!

After TikTok erupted, every other platform had its own version: Instagram released Reels, YouTube had Shorts. I transferred some of my TikTok videos onto Shorts, not expecting them to perform as well.

207

And, for the first few months, that was the case. So, I just left it all there and forgot about it.

Then, on a day when I was feeling burnt out and had no motivation, I decided to look at my YouTube channel, which I hadn't done for a few weeks. I now had 19,000 subscribers – up by three thousand! One of my Shorts was on half a million views. I was genuinely lost for words. Seeing that spurt of success gave me serious motivation, and made me realise you should never give up on things – because the moment you give up might be the moment you blow-up!

The next week was the craziest, busiest one of my life. I started posting five Shorts a day on YouTube, and the half-a-million-viewed video went to five million in the space of a day. It was always one of my biggest goals to succeed on YouTube, even before TikTok, Instagram and all the other platforms came along. Right back when I posted my very first 'Dan, Dan The Magic Man' video.

After that, things moved fast, and I gained a million subscribers in a week. Several of my videos reached the YouTube trending page, and one of them was trending number one in the entire world. The best thing about reaching a million subscribers was knowing that I'd now qualify for a YouTube creator award. As a kid, I used to see YouTubers unboxing their shiny creator awards, and now I had two on the way. One for reaching 100,000 subscribers and the other for passing a million.

While it was a real buzz knowing how many people were watching me, at the same time it sometimes felt like a lot of pressure. There was hardly a day when I could sit back and think, 'Oh, I won't bother posting anything today.' Instead, I felt like I had to deliver more and more. There were people from all over the world commenting on what I was doing, looking at my new videos every day, so I just felt like I had to keep going.

The funny thing was that the comments people left were split between positive and negative. As time went on, I actually started to notice quite a lot of hate toward me and the videos. It was quite a weird feeling, thinking that people were thinking nasty thoughts and saying horrible things about me when they didn't even know me. When someone posts hate under a person's content or on their feed, they must realise that there's every chance that the person they're being nasty about is going to see it. Sometimes, I'd respond to the hate with something like, 'Thanks, mate, have a nice day.'

Sometimes, that would be enough to shame the person who had commented into making an apology. 'Oh, sorry, I was only joking. I was just watching videos and making comments. I didn't mean anything by it!'

It made me realise that I mustn't take it personally because, at the end of the day, these people don't know who you are, so how can they hate you? It was just something I had to ride out in those first few months, when I started noticing a lot of it. I didn't let it get to me. As time went on, people seemed to get bored with it, maybe because I didn't bite back or react, and, after a while, the majority of interaction was upbeat and friendly.

When things started going well for me, it had felt like a natural thing to ask Grandad to appear in one of the videos for my YouTube channel. He'd always loved watching me perform tricks, and he was happy to do it. We ended up filming loads of stuff together, and he loved seeing the online reaction. Now that I was starting really to get attention on YouTube and TikTok, he read all the comments, things like 'I love your grandad' or 'Your grandad is awesome; he makes our day'.

After a while, he really got into it. 'Hey, Dan, I'm a bit of a celebrity online now, aren't I?' It made me laugh. He didn't go out of the house that much, but one day he stepped out and got recognised by some local kids.

'Ah! We know you! You're that bloke in Dan Rhodes' video. You're Dan's grandad!'

I knew he absolutely loved that moment of fame and public recognition, although he sometimes pretended it was all a bit of a bother. Sometimes, I'd turn up at his house, full of ideas, and he'd roll his eyes at me. 'What are you doing here again?' he'd say, as if he hated me bugging him. 'Not another bloody video!'

THESE PEOPLE DON'T KNOW WHO YOU ARE SO HOW CAN THEY HATE YOU?

Then, if I didn't call or go round there for a week, he'd be on the phone to me.

'Hey, Dan! When are we next filming some videos?'

My grandad was a real joker, so I've got a whole bunch of bloopers and outtakes, where he's just messing about and taking the mick.

'You're a crap magician, you,' he'd say. 'Why don't we try and find a proper magician to do it properly?'

Another person who's become a regular in my videos is Emily Berry. I first met Emily through Harrison – they'd been good friends since they were young. For a few years, Emily moved to Dubai, but when she came back, she reconnected with Harrison again, and came over to visit our house. I asked Emily if she'd just film a quick Instagram video with me while she was there. In that video, I gave her a staple gun that gave an electric shock when you pressed it. Nice!

The video did quite well as far as likes and views went, and luckily Emily wasn't in the least bit put off, even after being electrocuted. So,

Emily
ON DAN

I've been appearing in Dan's videos for quite some time now, and the more content he created, the more he'd ask me to be a part of it. I think he likes the way I react to the magic.

The funny thing is, however long I've done it, and however many videos I've appeared in, I'm genuinely surprised by what he does, every time. You'd think I'd see the secret behind the trick sometimes, sitting so close to him, but I really don't know how he does it. It's madness!

From the bottom of my heart, I think that Dan is such a great and humble person. It doesn't matter how much he achieves or how much success he has, he keeps going simply because he genuinely loves what he does. He wants to entertain people.

As well as that, he's very down to earth, and a good friend. When I'm with him, we'll spend half the time filming and the other half just talking: about my day, about his day, about where we see ourselves in five years – whatever comes up!

I think that's why his followers and subscribers relate to him, because he's likeable and personable. At the end of the day, he is just an eighteen-year-old boy doing magic in his bedroom, but the fact that he's been driven enough to turn that into a career is pretty amazing, I think!'

she agreed to film another video the next time she came over, and it kind of went from there. The best thing about Emily is how great and natural she is on camera, plus her reactions are mint – which is exactly what you need when you're doing magic. Gradually, we started to film more and more things together, and now Emily is a regular on my YouTube channel. One of our regular features is 'rate the magic trick', where I perform all sorts of tricks

using all manner of props, while Emily scores them out of ten. Some of my recent ones have involved shrinking a bottle of water, making a deck of cards float, and singeing a hole in Emily's jumper before making the burnt hole vanish so it's as good as new.

With the end of lockdown came a return to a bit of normality. Still, when you spend as much of your time locked in a room making and editing content as I do, it can sometimes be hard to notice the difference. One thing that has changed

since lockdown is that magic really has become my full-time career now. I have to be organised and disciplined with it, just like I would any other job. It's what I love doing and it's how I intend to make a living going forward.

TIPS FOR MASTERING SOCIAL MEDIA

These are my tips for mastering social media and becoming a fantastic and successful content maker.

1 Find Your Niche!

Anyone can make content and post videos, but it's a good idea to know what works for you. And if you don't know, find out! The stuff you love watching online may not necessarily be the thing you excel at. For instance, me putting out a dancing video would be a pretty terrible decision on my part, because I can't dance to save my life. If you can dance, though, dance! If you're funny, keep making people laugh. And if you're a fantastic singer... well, you know what to do.

The technical stuff

Like the performance side of things, the technical stuff is also a learning curve. It's a bit of trial and error and learning new skills, which is all part of the fun.

On a practical level, good lighting is always a key factor when you're making a video. Nobody wants to watch something that looks like it's shot in a dark shed. In the early days, I used to use natural light from my window, but these days I use a ring light, which is something you can pick up fairly cheaply and which does the job nicely.

You might want to use editing software. I use iMovie to edit my YouTube videos, but there are lots of different apps out there – just do an Internet search and decide what's best for you. To be honest, you can do so much on your smartphone these days, you don't really need a fancy set-up.

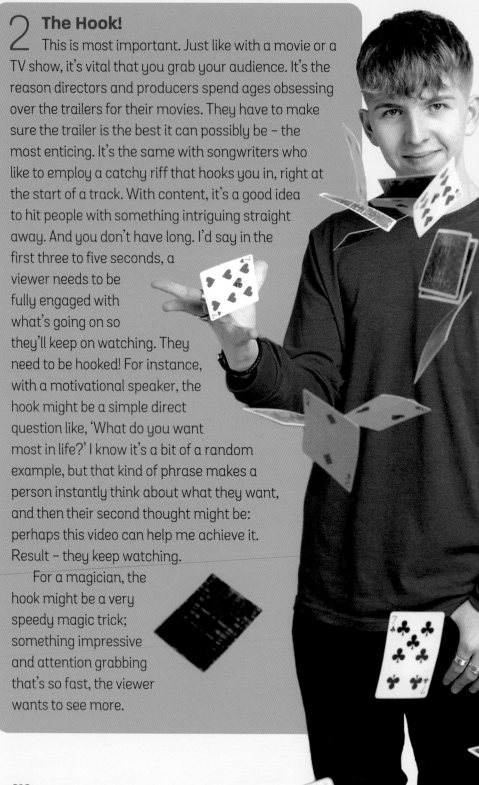

2 The Hook!

This is most important. Just like with a movie or a TV show, it's vital that you grab your audience. It's the reason directors and producers spend ages obsessing over the trailers for their movies. They have to make sure the trailer is the best it can possibly be – the most enticing. It's the same with songwriters who like to employ a catchy riff that hooks you in, right at the start of a track. With content, it's a good idea to hit people with something intriguing straight away. And you don't have long. I'd say in the first three to five seconds, a viewer needs to be fully engaged with what's going on so they'll keep on watching. They need to be hooked! For instance, with a motivational speaker, the hook might be a simple direct question like, 'What do you want most in life?' I know it's a bit of a random example, but that kind of phrase makes a person instantly think about what they want, and then their second thought might be: perhaps this video can help me achieve it. Result – they keep watching.

For a magician, the hook might be a very speedy magic trick; something impressive and attention grabbing that's so fast, the viewer wants to see more.

3 Kill Your Darlings!

This isn't as nasty as it sounds. What does it mean? Well, it also translates to cut off all the fat (actually, I'm not sure that sounds much better!). Anyway, what it means is, keep your videos succinct and snappy. The phrase 'kill your darlings' is often used by writers as a reminder that, however much they might love a certain line or paragraph or character, if those things are not moving the story forward, they have to go. If there's something there that doesn't help your story or the theme of your video, get rid of it, however clever or hilarious it might be. It's something I've had to learn over time and I've had to be ruthless.

These days, I might spend five or ten minutes working on a section of the video only to find that it doesn't really fit with the overall theme. So, I cut it out. It's always quite a good idea to watch your videos from the point of view of someone who doesn't know you. For instance, I'll watch mine back as if I'm someone who knows nothing about Dan Rhodes. I ask myself, if I didn't know who this person was and it was the first time I'd seen him, would I keep watching? It's true that your most loyal followers might watch you whatever, but if your goal is to build your audience, you have to stay on your toes when it comes to appealing to people who are new to you.

4 Add A Twist!

By that I mean end your video with something big, a climax that makes the video worth watching. Something that a viewer might not expect or see coming. If a video looks like it's hyping up to something really cool but then doesn't pay off at the end, the audience may not invest in what you're doing or be inclined to re-watch. I usually end my videos with a really cool trick and then cut the video off as soon as the trick is done. That way, people will often watch again, just to see that impressive bit at the end.

I decided to add my own twist to the end of our photoshoot!

5 Call To Action!

This is also a great way of engaging people when it comes to content. Saying something like, 'Guys, if you like this video, follow me for more.' Give your viewers the idea to hit the like button, or add a 'subscribe for more' text, right at the end.

6 Be Yourself and Have Fun!

Lastly, and very importantly, if you're doing what comes naturally and you look like you're having a good time, it will come across to the audience.

THE POPCORN TRICK

I love looking at what's around me, or picking something up in a shop, and thinking how I can make it into a trick, like this one where I make popcorn magically appear.

What you'll need: A paper plate, some popcorn, super glue, a marker, a cloth and a bowl. This one is as much about the preparation as it is the trick itself.

1 Put the bowl face down on the paper plate and trace around it with the marker.

2 Then cut around the circle – make sure you cut inside the line so there's no line visible on the cut-out section.

turn over →

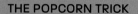

3 Superglue the popcorn to the circle so it looks like a nice healthy plateful and leave to dry – younger kids please do this with some adult supervision!

4 When you're ready to do the trick, conceal the popcorn circle under a cloth or paper towel and have it one side.

5 First hold up the empty bowl for your audience to see, then pick up the cloth, keeping the paper circle with the popcorn glued to it hidden behind. Lower the cloth over the bowl, dropping the circle of popcorn into the bowl as you go.

6 Whip the cloth away to create the illusion that the bowl has filled up with popcorn. It's quite an incredible visual, if I do say so myself!

THE ETERNAL PAPER BAG

This is one for social media! It's an incredible banger!

What you'll need: A paper bag, a pair of scissors, a bottle of juice or water, and a table.

shhh!!

1 Before you start the trick you'll need to cut a square hole in the back of the paper bag, then fold the bag up so you can't see it.

2 For the trick, you need to be sitting at the table with the bottle of juice hidden in your lap. Hold up the folded bag, showing both sides – because it's folded nobody can see the hole!

turn over →

3 Unfold the bag and put it on the table – with the hole side hidden – then open the bag and put your hand inside.

'll do this
things on
g one thing
another!
hy it's an
nal bag!

4 Reach down inside the bag, putting your hand through the hole. Grab the drink from your lap and pull it through the hole and out of the bag. It looks like you've pulled a drink from an empty bag!

THE DISAPPEARING CRAYONS

People are always amazed when you make something disappear, so this is a really cool one.

What you'll need: A box of crayons with an opening at the front, sticky tape.

1 Before you start filming the clip, take the crayons out of the box and snap them directly in half.

turn over →

2 Then tape the top halves of the crayons together, discarding the bottom halves.

3 To do the trick, put the crayons back in the box, squeezing the sides of the box against the crayons to hold them in place and in view. Show your audience the box of crayons, which looks full.

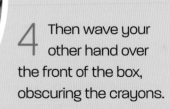

4 Then wave your other hand over the front of the box, obscuring the crayons.

5 Release pressure of your fingers on the box so the crayons fall to the bottom of the box, out of sight. The crayons have disappeared!

TURNING EIGHTEEN

These days, I'm posting four of five videos a day because I believe that consistency is key to maintaining a solid social media profile. I don't imagine that will change, especially if I want to keep growing.

A typical Dan Rhodes day goes something like this . . .

I prefer to wake up when I wake up. Unless I've got something specific that I have to be up for, I don't set an alarm. I actually stayed in bed until after midday today (you can see the work ethic right there!). Now my body clock is going to be all out of sync. Damn it! I actually prefer it when I can get to bed by about ten o'clock and then get up at seven, but it doesn't always work out when you've got a video to finish editing. It only takes one late night to throw it all out!

Once I'm fully conscious, I'll spend time talking to or messaging my friends, and then I'll eventually get going with making videos. As I said, it's hugely time-consuming and involves a fair bit of forethought and planning. Of course, as time has gone on, it's got easier. I've put out enough content now to know what I'm doing without getting bogged down with too many problems. Still, when you're doing that many videos a day, you have to be on it, so there's not a massive amount of time left for a social life. So, basically, I don't have one!

Actually, that's not totally true. I'm most definitely not a person who sits around doing nothing. It's important for me to always be moving forward, always aiming to achieve something. If I can, I'll go to some kind of magic event or show, just to keep an eye on what's happening. If I'm not making a video or making magic somewhere myself, any spare time I do have is for meeting up with friends.

You might think I stalked and found all my friends and collaborators from social media sites, but not so! Some of them I knew as actual real-life people!

I had friends from all over come to my eighteenth birthday party, a lot of them I'd met through doing magic or online, or social media. Emily was there too, and Harrison; my fellow magician and best pal Joel was also in attendance.

It was quite the occasion, held in the middle of some COVID-19 restrictions at a restaurant called The Late Lounge in Oldham. OK, so I was allowed to have a party at the time, but we all had to stay pretty much seated at tables. Either that or we could stand outside under the outdoor heaters. I wasn't going to let that spoil my enjoyment, though.

One of the guests at the party was one of my very newest friends, Gabriel Templar. Gabriel is a brilliant singer/songwriter, who I became a big fan of from watching his videos on TikTok. Gabriel's songs have an old-school vibe. He's influenced by a lot of music from the 1950s and 60s, but he gives it an indie-pop twist. I think it's a very original sound, and you should definitely check it out. It turned out that he'd been watching my videos too. So the appreciation was mutual, which is why we ended up messaging one another, then talking on FaceTime.

FRIENDS FROM ALL OVER CAME TO MY EIGHTEENTH BIRTHDAY PARTY

On the night of my birthday, I'd asked Gabriel to bring his guitar, and, of course, I got him to play and sing during the evening (at least until he broke a string!). Meanwhile, all sorts of magic was going on around the place while he played.

Now, I'm not a big fan of drinking alcohol, but because it was my eighteenth, all my friends insisted on buying me drinks. I thought it would be rude not to, really. Just this once! I didn't even know what

Gabriel
ON DAN

As much as I love music, I'm also kind of obsessed with anything magic related, so when I first discovered Dan on TikTok, I became a fan. Within a few days of following one another on socials, we were messaging and speaking on FaceTime.

It was quite weird really, because when we spoke, it was as if we'd known one another for ages. Then, when we finally met to do some filming together, with me providing a bit of musical commentary to his tricks, that feeling was even stronger. It's like we were old friends, and in that respect Dan's been brilliant. With us having social media in common, it's good to have someone to ask advice and compare notes with. He's so incredibly switched on with it, and we tend to think very similarly when it comes to that kind of thing.

There are definitely times with Dan when it's more intense than others – mainly because he's just so driven and motivated – but he's a genuinely lovely guy, and a great friend.

kind of drinks to have when they asked me. I think there were a couple of shots and maybe a gin in there to start with, but I wasn't too keen.

I do like blackcurrant cordial, so I was more than happy to switch to that. However, unbeknown to me, some of my mates had decided that there was no way I should be drinking fruit cordial at my eighteenth birthday party, so they decided to add some vodka secretly. Vodka and blackcurrant isn't the first drink that springs to mind, is it? This was my first time ever having more than one drink and, not being used to it, the alcohol went straight to my head. You can just imagine what I was like by the end of the night.

It was a fantastic night, but becoming an adult was a strange concept for me. Half the time, I still act like a kid. In my head, I'm eight, not eighteen!

Actually, I do sometimes feel like I should be looking after myself a bit more, so one of my 2022 New Year's resolutions was to get that sorted; maybe do some running or some gym stuff. OK, so it's not happened yet, but we're not that far into the year so please let me off. I'm also conscious of the fact that I eat too much junk food! I'm lucky, so far, I haven't really put on too much weight, but I'm well aware that things could change if I don't cool it with the takeaways occasionally. Your health is your wealth – right?

I might not have kept my New Year's resolutions (yet . . .) but I have fulfilled one of my biggest dreams already this year. I've always wanted to walk the red carpet at a big event. I've watched celebrities, musicians and actors do it over the years. So, like many young people, I'd imagined myself in that same situation. At the start of 2022, I got a call from a lady called Vivianne, who works for YouTube.

'I was just wondering, Dan, do you know what the BRIT Awards are?'

'YES. OF COURSE!'

'Well, I don't know whether it would be your thing, but we'd like to invite you to come along to the BRITs and to perform some magic tricks while you're walking the red carpet at the O2 Arena.'

OH MY GOD!!!! Can you imagine? I didn't need asking twice. Funnily enough, a few months prior to the BRITs, I'd messaged their official Instagram account, asking if I could perform magic at the ceremony someday. They didn't respond, but maybe I'd put it out into the universe and someone had heard?

So, on 8 February 2022, I packed some red-carpet-worthy clothes and headed to London.

I have to say, I've never seen so many celebrities and famous people in one place. It actually felt quite weird seeing them all in person, especially some of the really big stars. I think we sometimes forget that they're real people! Olivia Rodrigo, Ed Sheeran, Sam Fender, Courtney Cox (aka Monica from *Friends!*). There were stars everywhere I looked. When I reached the spot where all the press were taking pictures, I spun some cards in the air so that they could get a good shot.

'That's great, Dan. Can we get another one?'

'Yeah, let's have another like that!'

Obviously, that meant getting down on the floor and picking all the cards up, which took a bit of time. We did another shot, but then they wanted another – so down I went again to gather my cards up off the floor. This went on for another five or six times, so, in the end, I spent half my precious time on the red carpet on my hands and knees. I hadn't been expecting that, to be honest. Meanwhile, because they

I go to the Brits!

only have one person at a time in front of the press, I was totally holding up the proceedings. There was definitely some kind of celebrity build-up behind me.

I must admit, I'd felt a bit nervous beforehand, thinking that nobody would know who I was, and I'd just be standing there waving like an idiot while no one took any pictures. But that wasn't the case at all. Actually, I was surprised by how many people recognised me. It felt amazing.

Inside the O2, I was whisked off to the YouTube VIP suite, which was part a row of boxes at the top of the arena that you can watch the show from. This suite was quite a fancy one, and I was there with other prominent YouTubers. Very cool.

I'd grown up watching YouTubers like the Sidemen, who, for those of you don't know, are a group of guys who make videos of themselves doing all kinds of challenges, as well as sketches and video-game commentaries. These guys were some of the earliest YouTube stars in the UK, and have a combined total of over 130 million subscribers – and here I was in a VIP suite with Simon Minter, aka Miniminter, who was one of the founding Sidemen members. Also there, was Ali-A, real name

Alastair Aiken, who's a gaming YouTuber known for his *Fortnite* and *Call of Duty* vlogs. He's actually one of the highest-paid professional online gamers in the world! I was most definitely in prestigious company (and of course, I was showing them tricks throughout the evening!).

I absolutely loved the BRITs experience, it was fantastic, but I was knackered by the end of it. I even turned down an invitation to the after-party because I was just so tired. Not very rock n' roll, you might think. But yeah, that's me!

February 2022 also saw the return of the Blackpool Magic Convention, which is the biggest of its kind in the world. I've been going to the convention for years; it's always a been a highlight for me and is another place I have made friends. There's so much magic going on, everywhere you look, with about 5,000 magicians from all over the world their doing their stuff. There are shows throughout the day, demonstrations, stands where you can buy and sell magic tricks . . . It's an incredible atmosphere and I'd highly recommend going along to any budding magician – actually, I'd recommend this annual event to anyone, whether they're a magician or not.

Like everything else, the Blackpool Magic Convention was affected by the COVID-19 pandemic, so it hadn't gone ahead last year, but this year it was back on with a vengeance. I was dead excited, and I have to say, this was quite a momentous one for me. Why? Because I was about to hit a massive milestone in my career as a magician. One I'd been waiting for quite some time.

During the convention, many of the magicians stay, or at least hang out at, The Ruskin, which is a hotel in the heart of Blackpool. And, yes, that's where I was on the Sunday night, hanging out in the bar with friends and family, poised to hit 10 million YouTube subscribers!

It's funny, it was just a little bit over a year ago that I was sitting in my back garden as the moon came out, thinking about the 10,000 subscribers I had. I was quite proud of that at the time, but I remember thinking, I need to make it 10 million! Numbers were everything – they

were like my driving force! I saw them as a measure of all the hard work I was putting in. I told myself that it didn't matter how long it took, I was going to achieve my goal. I knew it took some people years to build up that kind of following, but still I was determined. I actually said it out loud to myself while looking up at the moon.

That night in Blackpool, at around 11 o'clock, I put on the electronic live counter and we all waited. When it hit the magic number, a cheer went up in the room and I popped the cork from a champagne bottle. It was the perfect time to reach that milestone, on the final day of the Blackpool convention, surrounded by friends, family and fellow magicians. It felt brilliant!

I'm not going to stop there. No way! I want to keep growing. I won't be retiring any time soon! How could I with so many people around the world subscribing to my YouTube channel? I suppose that 10 million mark was something I always knew I could achieve if I worked hard enough, but I never in my wildest dreams imagined it would happen in just a little over a year!

Exactly a week later, I also hit 10 million on TikTok. And now I've reached those milestones, I'm not so worried about numbers anymore. I've spent such a long time in the rut of thinking, 'I want to hit 2 million, I want to hit 5 million,' and so on. It was like being on a numbers treadmill! Now I'm just going to concentrate on making the best content I can; making my videos as entertaining as possible for all the people who have already subscribed. The followers will grow I'm sure, but for me it's not about that anymore . . . it's all about the magic.

my dreams came true

my amazing Grandad

Grandad was always such a big part of my life, so when he died very suddenly of a heart attack at the end of 2021, just as I was about to start writing this book, it was so shocking and sad. It felt like one day he was here, and the next, he'd just disappeared. I spoke about his passing on my Instagram page and YouTube, and posted a photo of us together.

There were thousands of comments, something like 8000, on my YouTube page; people expressing their sadness, sending condolences and telling me how much they loved my grandad. It meant a lot.

On the last video I made with my grandad, he was singing the Frankie Valli song 'Can't Take My Eyes Off You'. I captured him belting out the 'I love you, baby!' chorus. You know the one!

A short while after he passed away, I went on a cruise with my mum and Harrison. It was supposed to be a holiday for my mum's birthday, but had been cancelled because of COVID, so we'd waited a long time to finally go.

Just before we left for Miami to catch the cruise ship, I found the video of my grandad singing. It was bittersweet, making me happy and sad all at the same time. On the plane to Miami, I listened to the song on repeat on my AirPods – 'I love you, baby' – over and over.

It was my first time in Miami, so needless to say, I was pretty excited – even though it was tinged with sadness. We spent two days in Miami before getting on the ship, and during that time, I continued to play

the 'I love you, baby' song for Mum and Harrison. It was just this lovely thing to remind us of Grandad.

On the day we boarded the cruise, we walked toward the big blue door leading onto the ship, hearing nothing but the voices of excited passengers, but as the door opened and we stepped on, we were greeted by a band playing that song. Literally, they were right at the chorus as the doors opened and we stepped on. We all burst out crying on the spot. Later we decided it was a sign that he was somehow there with us.

The most important lesson I learned from my grandad is that materialistic things don't really mean anything when it comes down to it. Possessions and things are not what's important in life. He never wanted anything more than what he had. To him, the important thing was the relationships you have with other people.

Guys, it might sound clichéd, but your family and the people you care about are the most important thing in the world. Don't forget to tell them you love them, and make sure that you're there for them as much as you can be. Always treasure the moments you spend with them because that time doesn't last forever.

my insta post

'Well, what can I say. I'm in total shock. This morning, I received the most devastating news of my life. My best friend in the whole world, my grandad Steve, passed away. It sounds like a cliché, but my grandad was the kindest, most friendly, loving person you could ever have the pleasure of meeting.

Grandad, I will miss coming to your house every day and saying, "Come on you old fart, it's time to film some videos." But even more, I'll miss the pleasure of your company and listening to music with you.

Words can't express how much you meant to me, and I'm sure I'll see you again. Rest in absolute paradise, you beautiful human being.'

ANYTHING IS POSSIBLE

It's a dream of mine is to have my own TV series – on Netflix no less! I wouldn't just be doing tricks for the sake of it, I'd be performing these magical feats for people, with the reveal of the trick being tied to them receiving something wonderful. I guess if something like that took off, I might make enough money so that my parents can retire and relax a bit.

OK, so this might seem like a fairly big dream. But my belief is, if you really want something, or you want to reach a goal, you have to put in the hours. If you do, then anything is possible.

This is why it's so important to do something you love and enjoy, rather than doing something just because it might seem cool or impressive. So, if you're intending to spend hours, days, weeks, months doing something – you have to love it. If you don't, you'll most likely get bored and give up.

A few years back, I came across something called *The Secret*, a book and a film exploring the laws of attraction, encouraging people to visualise their goals clearly to attract what they want. The idea is that, if you want something badly enough, believe in it, and take the necessary steps to achieve it, you can do almost anything. Positive thoughts bring positive things.

For me, the mind is a magnet, and you should use it to attract the things you want in life. That's why I try my best not to listen to or give space to negativity. It doesn't help me achieve my goals or make me happy, so I avoid it as much as possible. Even when I feel like someone is being negative, I'll do my best to turn it around. Of course, it's not always possible, but sometimes you can – so it's best to try.

Whatever you're trying to achieve, always remember that you're standing on the shoulders of giants. Although it's vital to have your heroes and inspirations, it's equally important not to copy or imitate. There can only be one Dynamo, one David Blaine ... and yes ... one Daniel Rhodes! So, for anyone who's reading this, whether you're a magician, a singer or any other kind of performer – it's important to make sure there's only one of you! What I mean is, think about what makes you unique. What makes you stand out from the crowd? Once you know that, it can become an invaluable part of whatever you're doing. It's like a trademark.

One really cool thing happened a couple of years ago, when I was asked to go back and be a 'star judge' at my primary school talent show. My teacher Miss Gardiner thought that as a veteran of the talent show myself, it would be nice for me to go back and see what the kids were doing now. It's really nice to be thought of in that way, and I think inspiring others is one of the most important things if you're successful on any kind of social media platform or in the public eye.

As I've got older, I feel like I've grown and changed, and the traits associated with the diagnosis I was given all those years ago have become less prominent and less noticeable. If anything, my obsession with magic has helped to bring me out of myself and overcome the shyness I had in my early school days. And as I've said, in the end, I went the opposite way altogether, with me going up to anyone, anywhere and asking, 'Do you want to see a magic trick?'

I suppose you could say that I used my difference to my advantage. Rather than thinking of it as something that was going to hold me back, I found that certain aspects of it were helpful with a lot of the things I was trying to achieve. For instance, the fact that I would get so fixated on one particular thing came in very handy when I focused on making videos and getting my magic out into the world. If there was something new that I wanted to learn or to achieve, I could use that single-mindedness and determination to really focus and help me get there. In that respect, my diagnosis wasn't so much of a disorder – more of a superpower! So there you go! Maybe Santa did secretly give me those superpowers back in Lapland all those years ago after all!

WRITE DOWN YOUR FUTURE GOALS

Acknowledgements

I'd like to thank myself for always believing in me (haha).

Thank you so much to my Grandad Stephen for all the amazing memories we created together, and for always believing in our journey. I miss you every single day. You were, and always will be, my best friend.

To my mother, where do I even begin? Thank you so much for always believing in me and working so hard to help me realise my dreams. I genuinely couldn't have done anything without you. Thank you for being the best mum I could ever ask for. Love you to the moon and back.

To my dad, thank you for making sure my determination to succeed never slowed :) Thanks for being the best dad in the world. Love you lots.

Thanks to my brother, Harrison, for being a constant pain in the a**e. (Seriously, thanks for always being a great brother to me and being my best friend growing up.)

To my Granny Cherelyn, I love you so, so, so much, you are the kindest woman on planet earth, thanks for everything.

To my Granny Barbara, love you lots

To my Great Granny Margaret, I miss you every day. I will never forget the time we had together and I will remember you until the day I die. Love you lots.

To Grandad John, thanks so much for being a fantastic grandad to me

To my little cousin Evie-Mae, love you very much. Hopefully you'll give this book a read :)

To Felan Davidson and Martin O'Shea, thanks so much for believing in me and massive credit to you both for being able to put up with me moaning all the time :). To Kate O'Shea and all the brilliant Bold Management team, thank you for being the best management in the world and for looking after me.

Dynamo, thank you so much for sparking my love for magic, you've been a true inspiration to me through the years and I'd love to think that in some small way I'm following in your footsteps

To Tom Bolton, thanks being one of my best pals! You're magic!

To Ash, thanks for being a legend, love you lots!

David Blaine, thanks for the inspiration

Mr Joel M . . . thank you so, so much for everything you have done for me. I consider you my greatest friend and it's a true honour to be friends with my hero.

My teachers, Mr Hollis, Miss Gardener and Mr Charnley, thank you so much each of you for having such a positive impact on my life.

Sarah Emsley and her amazing team at Headline Books, it's always been one of my biggest dreams to write a book and you guys made that possible, for that I will forever be grateful

Vivian at YouTube, thanks so much to you and your team. I'm still overwhelmed at what my YouTube channel has become, dreams really do come true.

To Emily, I genuinely couldn't have done what I've done without your help on the videos, it's always so much fun to have a laugh filming with you.

To Luca Gallone, you saw something in me when I had no followers to my name, I will always appreciate the help and advice you gave me, much love, mate.

Julius Dein, to the man who told me I could achieve my dreams all those years ago, thanks so much for believing in me and inspiring me to create content.

Gabriel Templar, Mr Templar, you are a hero and my favourite singer in the entire world and one of my closest friends. You are going to be a star.

My friend Vincent, thank you for all the memories. Being in *Charlie and the Chocolate Factory* was one of the best experiences of my life and I'm so glad we are still pals to this day.

Luke Osey, thanks for being a great friend.

To my friend, Elikir, so proud to see how well you have done. Keep killing it with YouTube.

Mark the Magician, thanks so much for helping me out when I was a young kid and showing me kindness and believing in me. I've got a little gift for you, which I'll send with this book.

To Shailen, thank you so much for all your help and advice over the last few years, I really do appreciate it.

LIFE IS
MAGIC